STORIES FROM THE OTHER SIDE

GORDON SMITH
with Chris Hutchins

HAY HOUSE

Australia • Canada • Hong Kong
South Africa • United Kingdom • United States

First published and distributed in the United Kingdom by:
Hay House UK Ltd, 292B Kensal Rd, London W10 5BE.
Tel.: (44) 20 8962 1230; Fax: (44) 20 8962 1239. www.hayhouse.co.uk

Published and distributed in the United States of America by:
Hay House, Inc., PO Box 5100, Carlsbad, CA 92018-5100. Tel.: (1) 760 431 7695
or (800) 654 5126; Fax (1) 760 431 6948 or (800) 650 5115. www.hayhouse.com

Published and distributed in Australia by:
Hay House Australia Ltd, 18/36 Ralph St, Alexandria NSW 2015.
Tel.: (61) 2 9669 4299; Fax: (61) 2 9669 4144. www.hayhouse.com.au

Published and distributed in the Republic of South Africa by:
Hay House SA (Pty), Ltd, PO Box 990, Witkoppen 2068.
Tel./Fax: (27) 11 706 6612. orders@psdprom.co.za

Distributed in Canada by:
Raincoast, 9050 Shaughnessy St, Vancouver, BC V6P 6E5.
Tel.: (1) 604 323 7100; Fax: (1) 604 323 2600

09 08 07 06 5 4 3 2 1
1st printing, September 2006
A catalogue record for this book is available from the British Library.

ISBN 1-4019-1172-2
ISBN 978-1-4019-1172-0

Printed and bound in Great Britain by TJ International, Padstow, Cornwall.

Foreword

I WAS lying on a beach in Thailand when the message came through (not from the Spirit world, I hasten to add) on my mobile phone. Would I like to assist the medium Gordon Smith in writing this book? I had time on my hands and he had precious little so it seemed like a good idea. My wife was against it: she said, 'You know absolutely nothing about the Spirit world.' And she was right: my previous books had been biographies of the royal family, showbusiness stars like Tom Jones and The Beatles, and billionaires such as Roman Abramovich and Sir James Goldsmith.

I write that at the outset because I feel it is important to make it clear that I came to this project with a completely open mind. I was neither a believer nor a non-believer. But I was certainly interested in what a man like Gordon Smith – hailed by the *Daily Mail* as 'Britain's most accurate medium' – could do and how he did it.

For me, it turned out to be the start of another incredible journey. I saw and heard things that I could not explain and knew of no-one else who could – and that includes Gordon himself.

In April I set out with him on a tour of British cities. To watch him step up on stage for three hours with no script to read, no lyrics to sing and no instrument to play, was in itself an astonishing experience. Yet this man, who had kept up his work as a Glasgow barber until shortly before the tour began, showed no sign of nerves. He had total faith that his Gift would see him through. And, as I can testify, it did. Every night.

I will leave it to him to recount on the ensuing pages many of the stories he has to tell of messages from the Other Side, save one: On the last night of the tour he was playing to yet another full house when something seemed to go wrong. He had a message for the mother of a teenage boy who had died of something that had happened to his head. But the lady he was delivering it to seemed confused. She could not relate to the information she was being given.

At that point Gordon realized that he had not made contact with the right person – his messenger indicated that he was in the wrong row. He was directed instead to an Indian lady seated immediately behind the first woman, who began to cry uncontrollably. When she recovered her composure she said: 'A few minutes ago I asked my son for a sign; "If you are here knock something over," is what I said to him in my silent prayer and at that moment the lady sitting beside me spilled her drink.'

She seemed surprised; Gordon wasn't.

We had driven into the town for the first time just a couple of hours earlier and to my certain knowledge Gordon had met no-one other than the stage doorkeeper and yet here he was once again giving accurate information to a total stranger about a loved one who had died. He told her that the first anniversary of her son's death was to be in a few days –

he was right – and that someone was preparing a memorial to the boy – right again: the boy's school had arranged a ceremony to consecrate a stone in his memory.

And so it went on. She screamed, 'Yes, yes, yes!' every time he told her something about that boy, for he was deadly accurate (no pun intended). Finally he delivered this message: 'Your son says, "Don't let my death ruin your life and please put away those thoughts of killing yourself."'

At the end of the night I saw the woman and her husband approach Gordon. She was sobbing and laughing at the same time and I heard her say to him: 'My husband doesn't even know this, but if my son hadn't come through tonight I was going to kill myself tomorrow. Everything you told me was accurate and I know now that his Spirit is living. Thank you, thank you, thank you.'

At that point her husband turned to me and said, 'Gordon Smith has saved my wife's life. She came here so miserable and she is going away so happy. She knows now that there is life on the Other Side and our son is living it.'

At this point it became clear to me that I was dealing with a truly remarkable man. In our conversations he has been totally open and honest about his own life and I have encouraged him to hold nothing back that will help people to know him better.

How can anyone argue with that?

Chris Hutchins, June 2006

Preface

I was very glad to be asked to write *Stories from the Other Side*, as it gave me a great opportunity to express myself to the reader. I have shared more of my personal life in this book than in any before – that in itself is very cathartic and a form of healing for any writer.

Writing about my life in this way would have been tough, but being offered the chance to work with Chris Hutchins made it much easier. Chris has written about people such as the Duchess of York, Elvis Presley and The Beatles, to name but a few.

Even more interesting for me was the fact that Chris came to this subject with no belief in mediumship, and I found it inspiring to watch him observe some of the people who came to me for help or healing.

I believe that the experiences Chris shared while working with me gave him something to consider when it comes to looking at life after death and life in this world.

It is also my wish that any who read this book will be given a chance to see the Other Side as I do, as a place of hope and peace and freedom from the suffering of this material world.

Peace be with you,
Gordon Smith

Acknowledgements

I would like to give special thanks to Chris Hutchins for his invaluable help in writing this book.

Grateful thanks also to Michelle Pilley and Jo Lal at Hay House for their hard work and support.

As always, thank you to all my family.

Contents

1

Who Am I ...?

NOTHING, they say, happens in God's world by accident or by mistake. And nothing bears out that maxim more clearly than the account of my very first visit to a Spiritualist church and hence the start of this amazing journey I am on. So allow me to begin this tome by recording the amazing sequel to a story I told at the start of my first book, *Spirit Messenger*.

Readers of that offering may recall the story of Christine Peebles, an old school chum who went on to work with me in a Glasgow hairdressing salon. Her brother Brian – also a friend of mine – died in a fire at the apartment they had bought together in the West End of Glasgow and had appeared to me in visionary form at the precise moment of his death some miles away. After the funeral I asked Christine if there was anything I could do to help her overcome her grief and she said she would like to go to a Spiritualist church to see if a medium could give her news of Brian from the Other Side. I thought it was a daft idea but this was no time to argue so I made a few calls, located the Glasgow Association of Spiritualists in Somerset Place and duly accompanied Christine to a service. There a medium called Mary Duffy gave messages to both Christine and me: hers was that she should try and locate a medium called Albert

Best (whom neither of us had ever heard of) and he would deliver a message when the time was right. If that message surprised Christine then the one I was to receive astonished me: Mary said that my late grandmother had come through and was telling her that I would become a medium myself.

Now for that amazing sequel. I did, of course, become a medium just as grandmother, via Mary Duffy, had foretold. Ten years later I was entertaining a group of friends, who now included the aforesaid Albert Best, to drinks in my flat. Albert, whom I had never told of Mary's message to Christine, said, out of the blue, 'Who is Brian who died in a fire? I can smell smoke and I have a message from him.'

'Leave it, Albert,' I said. 'This is a social occasion.' But he persisted: 'The message is not for you, in fact this message is for a young woman who will arrive here tonight.' I was puzzled. It was pretty clear he was talking about Brian Peebles but Christine had married and moved on in the intervening decade and I happened to know that she was on holiday on the Isle of Mull. It wasn't long, however, before the telephone rang, and no prizes for guessing that the caller was Christine. She had just made the long journey back to Glasgow and, although she was tired, she said she felt an overwhelming urge to come over and see me. I didn't mention this to Albert and less than an hour later my school friend walked through the door. I told her to go and help herself to a drink but as she passed Albert in his corner chair he said, 'You're Christine, aren't you? We have never met but my name is Albert Best.' And with that he asked the rest of us to leave the room. Minutes later Christine emerged in floods of tears and, throwing her arms around me, said, 'Gordon, I got my brother back tonight.' She was closely followed by Albert who looked drained and merely said, 'Will somebody get me a drink?'

If ever I am in doubt about the work I do, I look back on such events for which I have not been responsible and my faith sweeps back in with joyous force.

*****

ONE has to admit that 'Gordon Smith' is about as ordinary as names go. But then I like to think I'm a pretty ordinary fellow. I like a good drink at the end of the day, smoke far more cigarettes than a doctor would say is good for me, and enjoy most of the pleasures this life has to offer. So there is not much that marks me out from the next fellow.

Except, that is, for The Gift, this unexplainable Gift that allows me to communicate with the Spirit world and help people who are overcome by grief by relaying messages from those who have moved on from this life. In this book you will find many extraordinary stories. Let me say at the outset that they are as amazing to me as they probably will be to you. I never cease to be surprised by what The Gift produces, by what the Spirits tell me to pass on and the effect it can have on its beneficiaries. And as frank as they have been with me – on both sides, that is – I intend to hide nothing about myself and my own journey through this life.

There is nothing extraordinary about my background, although – as a result of what I was clearly born to do – my life today is very different to the one I was born to. Mansel Street in the Springburn district of Glasgow was not considered to be a wild street, but the area of Springburn was in places quite rough. I didn't realize it at the time because it's only when you move on and look at other people's backgrounds that you see that my childhood experiences were clearly not part of everyone's upbringing.

My parents, Sammy and Liz, had moved out of the Gorbels and gone to live in Easterhouse before moving to Springburn in the north of the city. These were all areas where you had to be pretty tough to survive and that probably moulded their characters. We were a big family – like my father before me, I was one of seven children, although in my case I was the youngest and well-protected by my siblings. I can remember witnessing street fights when I was young – usually fuelled by alcohol because in those days in Glasgow the drink laws were so tight. Pubs closed at nine o'clock each night, so all the men got drunk on shorts just beforehand, really putting it away on top of all the pints they'd already supped. My father was not a great drinker but he was a man's man and he'd have a few pints before he came home.

My mother, on the other hand, hated alcohol and blamed the world's troubles on it. On my mother's wedding night her mother choked to death in her bed after a few drinks and instead of setting off with my dad on the first day of their married life, Mum had to arrange a funeral and become an instant mother to her siblings because my father was off with the Navy.

So from the age of 19, my mother was left to bring up a young family on her own in the Gorbels – a very rough part of Glasgow in those days – so she had to be tough to protect her younger siblings.

My father – a builder, by the way – is only 5ft 6in and not at all wild but he's sturdy and can handle himself. He was never like the wild Gorbels men who used knives. The honourable way for men to settle their differences was to go to the Glasgow Green, strip to the waist and fight man-to-man – what we called a 'square go' – and that's what my father did if he had to.

Growing up in no. 97 Mansel Street was often very noisy – I suppose that we were a headstrong lot. Often fights would occur among us, but my mother was always capable of putting an end to them. The same applied if we had any trouble from other people in our area. Mum would defend her brood to the end; and people around got the message that you didn't mess with our family.

In my mother's eyes her family could never do anything wrong or if they did it was no-one's job but hers to sort it, so as I was growing up it was inevitable that I saw a great deal of violence. It wasn't uncommon for me to hear stories of people from the Gorbels being involved in violent episodes. People preferred to settle things without involving the law. I think that all of my family could handle themselves, which was fortunate for me as, being the youngest, I didn't really have to – I always felt protected.

As I look back over this I find much of the violence in Glasgow during my childhood came from the mix of differences between the Protestants and Catholics – issues which in those days were very apparent. This and poverty mixed with alcohol caused many of the senseless fights among people, fights I could never understand. On reflection, my abhorrence of violence and anger comes from watching people abuse one another over things which always seemed unimportant to me.

Even in our family there were many such outbursts between different sides, when my mother's and father's families would come together at weddings, funerals and other get-togethers. Mum's family were Catholic and strong followers of Glasgow Celtic; and Dad's family were Protestant and strictly Rangers supporters – I say this because in my mind as a child I assumed that these football teams had some bearing on religion. Put people from each side together, mix in some booze at an emotional event and bingo – the place might erupt. It wasn't only in my family – I noticed that many of my friends had similar upbringings; it's just how it was.

I put all of this on the record to show where I'm coming from. It made me quite a nervous child and I would go into my own little world as much as I could – and what an unusual world that proved to be. Thoughts came into my head – many of them premonitions – about things which I could not possibly have known. My eldest brother Tommy remembers me as a six-year-old playing behind the couch (a favourite hiding place) with my toys when my mother entered the room and said, 'Has anyone seen Joan? She should be home by now.' And without looking up from the toys I replied, 'She's in Carlisle police station.'

I was chastised for making such an absurd utterance but within an hour the police had phoned from Carlisle to say they had Joan at their station having just rescued her from a broken-down car. Tommy still says today that he and Betty believed I was making up all the unexplainable things that I came out with. So I stopped telling them things and retreated further into my very deep inner world. These were wilful people who had to finish what they were doing before they took notice of what must have sounded like strange rantings from a small child.

We didn't see much of my father. He worked every hour that God sent – both he and my mother liked a good home and everything they had was bought and paid for; neither liked debt. We were the first family in the street to have a colour TV and my father had built many special features in our house – so much so that lots of the neighbours would come in to see his new creations.

My brothers Tommy and Sammy are both very talented artists and my sister Betty, like my mother, was a very good singer. I can remember her practising in her bedroom for singing competitions when I was young. In fact I think we all lived to sing and entertain each other.

Music was always playing in the background from the big old record player in my older brothers' and sisters' bedrooms, usually Tamla Motown stuff I remember – and I can still see Betty getting ready and holding a hairbrush in her hand in front of her mirror singing along to the Supremes before going off to sing with a girl group she was in.

Even at funerals there would be a singing competition. Like all good Glasgow funerals and weddings, after the fight there would be a singalong. When my grandfather died I remember both branches of the family being present. My mother's father was Catholic, so mostly that side was gathered in the bedroom where his body was laid out, but one of the Protestant side caused some uproar by offending their religion and all hell broke loose – the strange thing was that in no time at all, all of the same people were sitting together drinking and encouraging one another to sing their favourite songs and laments. There really is nowt so queer as folk!

*****

AS a child I never thought about death. When my grandfather died, the reaction of others puzzled me. I couldn't understand why my mother let out a scream when she discovered he had passed in the next room where she had been nursing him. My brother and I were playing with football things in the hall and I remember running into the room and seeing him, just looking at him. I wasn't frightened and shortly afterwards I took over his bedroom. My older brothers were shocked that I didn't mind being in a room where a dead man had been but even back then (and I was only nine) death held no fear for me; as it does not today, of course.

A lot of people say it was because I had already been having some kind of psychic experiences by then that I wasn't affected by death. But that's not the answer. You have an experience that's different and you don't know it's different until somebody points that out so I couldn't say I was psychic because I wouldn't have had the faintest idea what that meant.

My mother remembers that she had the first inkling of my powers when I was just four years old. She was bringing me back from a shopping trip and when we reached the house she put the key in the door and I screamed and told her not to go in. 'Nonsense,' she said but she was very wary nevertheless as she entered the house, checking each room in turn. I was whimpering because I sensed there was something bad there. Finally, when Mum entered the bedroom she realized there was someone there. A man was hiding under the bed after being disturbed in mid-burglary. This was a man who lived in our area and I'm sure I heard whispers that my brother took matters into his own hands – but no police were called. Something else I remember was that if our family could sort something out then the police were never an option.

Probably the first meaningful psychic experience I had was when I was seven. That's when I experienced what we in the psychic world call a materialisation. Ummy, a friend of my mother and father's, used to visit us after he'd had a good drink and when he came out us kids would gather round knowing he would give us pennies. One day I saw him walking along the street towards me and he stopped for a bit of a chat. Then he started to sing a little song I'd never heard before but was all about a place on the other side of town called Dalbeth.

I went home and told Mum I'd seen Ummy, who had talked to me and sung me the song and she freaked out. It turned out that the man had died two weeks earlier and was buried in Dalbeth cemetery. I can see now that it was made all the more traumatic for her because when they had found his battered body no-one could work out whether he'd fallen off a bus, been hit by a car or beaten up when he was drunk, and that's why they hadn't liked to tell me about his death. The look on her face was one of horror and I ran away because of it – not because I'd just seen my first 'ghost', I mean, he wasn't see-through or anything like that – but because Mum was acting so strange about it.

There were numerous occasions when I remember seeing people walking around my bedroom at night. It was a bedroom I shared with Sammy and John. I didn't want to get up and more than once I wet the bed rather than going to the toilet. It wasn't that I was frightened; I just felt the room was really busy and I shouldn't disturb them. It's hard to explain that to people unless they've experienced a similar feeling (and few, it seems, have) but I would be woken up in the middle of the night and often I would hear people talking. They would just be shadowy figures with a kind of pale golden light around them. I felt more like *I* was the intruder than they were.

I was fascinated by this yellowy golden mist that accompanies Spirits. I still occasionally see them today but now I can tell them, 'Go away, I want to sleep.' In those days I just didn't dare to do that, I didn't want to get in the way. When I did venture down the passageway to the toilet I would see more of them and I really did feel as if I was in their way.

None of this struck me as strange. I was unaware that it never happened to other members of my family or friends because I was discouraged from talking about such things. And don't get me wrong, I wasn't drawn to anything macabre like horror films or ghost stories, I was more into music.

By the time I was nine I knew the words of just about every Tamla Motown hit on the charts (that's still my favourite music). Tommy must take the credit for that. He would take me to the local record shop, install me in a sound booth seated on the shelf with a pair of headphones on, and leave me for an hour or two while he went to The

Lunar Seven, a nearby pub, to drink with his fellow Mods. So I could duet with Marvin Gaye, the Temptations and the Four Tops when I was still at primary school. I never had time for anything but the real thing and that did not include Elvis Presley whom even at that early age I regarded as a pseudo black singer. At home I would join in when Betty and Joan were singing *Heard It Through The Grapevine*, *Can't Hurry Love* or *My Girl*.

*****

AS I am writing this I am recalling a dream I had last night, which is relevant to this period of my life. It was a most bizarre dream in which a medium I know appeared, saying, 'Remember the 17th.' Now as it happens the 17th is a very significant date in that five or six of the people closest to me have their birthdays on that day of the month, but my mind was drawn to events on 17th September 1971 when I was just nine years old.

I was at a kids' party to celebrate the second birthday of my sister Betty's daughter Michelle. My brother Sammy was out with a crowd of his friends cycling in the hills just beyond Springburn. Most of the kids at the party were younger than me and I couldn't be bothered to join in the games so I sat in a corner on my own without any interference from the adults because they knew that's how I usually liked to be. I just sat there drifting when I saw the strangest thing: a boy pushing a bicycle walked straight through the wall. I knew who it was, it was Johnny Walker, one of Sammy's friends. He never smiled; he just stood there holding his bike and looking at me, and I remember thinking to myself, 'The party's over, it's finished.'

The next thing I knew my mother came running into the house, saying, 'Oh my God. A boy's been killed.' I remember Betty gasping and children screeching hysterically. It was, of course, Johnny Walker who had died. He and the other boys – they were all teenagers – had been out in the country and Johnny had left the group to push his bike across the road and get a drink of water from the pump and well outside a cemetery. A car had come round the corner at great speed and Johnny had been run over. This had taken place at the very same time I saw him walk through that wall. He didn't look happy and he didn't look sad; he'd just stared at me.

In those days my mother would gather up the black handbag she kept for such occasions and go knocking on neighbours' doors to collect whatever money they could spare for the boy's family. I went with her but I never did tell her about the vision I'd seen in the midst of Michelle's birthday party.

*****

NOT all of my early life was spent in the wild urban jungle that was Glasgow. I spent a happy chunk of it in the relative splendour of the south London suburbs with my mother's younger brother Michael, his wife Sylvia and their son Stephen. Michael had moved his family south some years earlier and set up a successful roofing company so they were pretty well-off. Michael was a headstrong man, but Sylvia – a real lady – seemed just about able to keep him in check. Their mock Tudor house on a tree-lined road was the height of luxury for a lad from a big family from a council house in Glasgow. Cousin Stephen and I got taken out for meals at places like the local Berni Inn, and that certainly never happened in Glasgow. I had my own room at Michael and Sylvia's place and we even went away on holiday. It was only to a south coast holiday camp but to me it was schoolboy heaven.

There was, however, a tragic reason for my continued presence in their household. Stephen had been diagnosed with cancer and didn't have that much time left to live. In short, I was there as a dying boy's companion. I wasn't at the house when he died – I had been sent home when he was in the last throes of his illness – and I remember that early one Sunday morning my father got a phone call. I could tell from the tone of his voice that he was being told Stephen had passed over.

After the funeral Aunt Sylvia asked my mother if I could stay with them. At first Mum was a bit reluctant to let me be there with this grieving woman because Sylvia clearly regarded me as a substitute for the son she had lost. But she gave in and I was duly installed in Stephen's bedroom where I would play with his toys, sensing that he was very much there with me. I'd hold conversations with him and when I was making things with Lego I would hear him say, 'Oh, I could make it better than that!' – a claim which I would loudly dispute.

Aunt Sylvia would just hear fragments of the conversation and wonder whom I was talking to but when she put two and two together she would say, 'Oh my God, he's actually having conversations with Stephen.' But she told me some time later that far from being frightening she found that comforting. It was kind of subliminal; that was the weirdest part of it. I couldn't say it was graphic in the sense that I could actually see him, it was just the sense of feeling him around me and having conversations with him. I remember that so clearly. It was the first time I heard the voice of a Spirit.

In bed at nights I would be woken by the sound of his voice and I would say, 'Oh, what time is it, Stephen?' At that early age I could feel the Spirits actually bumping into me. Then, I suppose, they were preparing me for what lay ahead. Now it's more a case of feeling their pain, knowing what caused their earthly death if, say, it was a head injury, stomach cancer, heart attack, or just the body giving up from old age.

*****

I OFTEN look back on these events in my own early days when I am telling people who are complete strangers to me facts about their own lives which I could not possibly know without The Gift. Whether it be a one-to-one sitting or a demonstration in a packed theatre or concert hall, I get immense pleasure from seeing those who arrived beset with grief, leaving with joyous smiles on their faces as a result of what I have been able to pass on to them.

I also get surprised and sometimes amused by the way things sometimes turn out.

For example, it's interesting what mementos of loved ones those who come to me for one-to-ones sometimes bring along. A lady from Yorkshire, who recently travelled to London to see me, placed a biscuit tin on the table between us. Her husband Harry had died in 2005 and came through very quickly. He said he had been in hospital and returned home seemingly well, before dying very suddenly. Yes, she said, that was correct. He was talking about being there in December for his son's 15th birthday. Now at that point even the wife's mother – a sceptical woman who had accompanied her – let out a gasp. Clearly the evidence was right again.

He was mentioning a 'David' and the woman said, 'That's my other son.'

'*One* of your other sons,' I said. 'He's telling me you have four – four sons but no daughters and he's saying, "Give my love to all the boys."'

Then he said something which clearly amused both women: 'He's saying "Stop fooling around trying to get in touch with me."' She laughed and explained, 'It was my birthday the other day and I sat at the kitchen table with a pen in my hand and a piece of paper in front of me. I asked him if he was there to guide my hand and write something. "Please, please, give me a sign that you are there."'

'I know,' I said. 'He's saying he was there, laughing at you. What's more he had tried to give you a sign by messing about with the electrics in the house.' To which she responded, 'Well, somebody did – and he had been an electrician.'

And finally I told her that she should dispose of his ashes – they weren't even in an urn. 'I know,' she said, crying gently now. 'They're in there.' And she pointed at the biscuit tin on the table.

2

A Birth Changes Everything

WHEN I was growing up my one constant companion was a dog. Lassie – a small, clearly abandoned Irish setter puppy that followed me home from a country walk when I was no more than six or seven – knew all my secrets. She shared my hidden world. I was mortified when she reached the painful end of her life and had to be put down. But I had plenty of contact with her after that. She knew all about the Spirit world and wasted no time in coming forward, as have all the pets I've had – as we shall see.

I thought about Lassie when a lady came to see me just recently for a one-to-one. She wanted contact with her parents and she was not to be disappointed – both came through and gave her wonderful messages as well as evidence that it was indeed them. I was able to tell her that her father's name was Geoffrey and that I saw him in military uniform. The name was correct and she said he had been a captain in the Army. Her mother Dorothy described someone jumping with horses and my sitter subsequently explained that her daughter was a prize-winning showjumper.

But the strongest sense I got was from animals. I saw a most beautiful horse galloping around with a green Tara (a Tibetan deity) above her head and a large Labrador-type dog.

'He gives you protection,' I said. 'He's a Spirit animal. You have seen things happening around you and that's the love from these animals, the feelings that you get [relating to them] are these animals coming through. They talk to you, they never forget you.'

I told her I sensed the word Toby. She was incredulous. Tara was the stable name of a much-loved mare her daughter had lost the previous year and, she said, 'Toby was a large, loveable cross-breed we lost and buried in the garden – I always put flowers on his grave.'

Tara and Toby brought memories of Lassie flooding back to me. I had always felt somewhat guilty that in my teenage years I had become obsessed with sporting activities and had not, perhaps, paid her as much attention as she would have liked. But then, these were lean times for me spiritually too.

As a teenager I had developed a very healthy interest in all sports. All the family did. We were very competitive and still are. My father had been a superb athlete and encouraged us to take part in all manner of sporting activities and that included football, boxing, swimming, tennis and all forms of athletics. I specially loved gymnastics which none of the others had done before.

Mind you, my parents never really got involved with their kids' sporting achievements and even when I was in the finals of the Scottish gymnastics championships only Tommy came along to see me. That didn't particularly bother me because I knew Mum and Dad were both very busy and an amateur event didn't count for much in our family.

Now, if I'd been a professional footballer … but, alas, that was not to be. Like other local kids I followed the fortunes of Celtic and Rangers and was mesmerized by the players' lifestyles. On many occasions I have helped football stars, but when they come to me they are in need of help. All the magic they bring to the football pitch means nothing when they've suffered a great loss in their life.

But I digress. When I was 17 I was picked for Scotland's squad for the Commonwealth Games. I must confess I didn't really want to go. The games were being held in New Zealand and despite all the ructions at home I wasn't keen to be that far away from my family, so I saw it as a godsend when I broke my hand and had to pull out.

However, it's true to say that every minute of my spare time in those days was devoted to sport. There were sports camps, weekend camps and training nights. You didn't dare smoke or drink on that programme and discos were a definite no-no, so I didn't see much of the pals I had grown up with. Inevitably that meant that my experience with girls was limited and when I first cast eyes on Kate Gargano I have to admit that there was something special that drew me to her good looks, blonde hair (which defied her Italian origins) and tremendous figure. We met up frequently in the neighbourhood (Kate had recently moved to Springburn) and formed a relationship very quickly.

Like all my brothers who brought home girlfriends, my mother never thought they were good enough for her sons. But that didn't bother Kate; she's quite strong and stood up to my mother, who presumably thought, 'You're stubborn, you're not going to go away, so I suppose I'll have to go along with it.'

I never did propose to her. Kate got pregnant and that decided it. The moment our eldest son, Paul, was born on

15th June 1981 changed a lot of things. For one, I started smoking. There was another fellow in the hospital waiting room smoking cigarette after cigarette and when he offered me one, the natural thing to do seemed to be to accept it.

Paul's birth at Stobhill was amazing. Neither Kate nor I had reached our twentieth birthdays and up until he was delivered I remember being somewhat embarrassed at even being in a hospital maternity department. I had no confidence in myself as a father and potential husband. The nurse asked me if I wanted to go in and watch the birth and I said, 'No.' Then, once he was born, they called me in and when I saw him for the very first time, things changed. His eyes were so dark and he had loads of dark hair. The midwife was singing a song called *One Day In Your Life* which Michael Jackson had high in the charts at the time and I just felt this amazing rush and my eyes filled with tears. I knew my life would never be the same again. I had grown up in an instant.

It was four in the morning and I dashed to the phone to call all the people I had promised to let know when the baby arrived, but even though I had been ringing those numbers all the previous evening to report developments, now I couldn't remember a single one of them and had to keep calling back to directory inquiries.

That done, I went out and bought my first packet of Benson & Hedges. I was hooked on more than fatherhood.

Sometime afterwards Kate and I got married. We were both absolutely skint and as an apprentice hairdresser I was earning practically nothing, but we somehow managed to get a council flat close to Mansel Street so it seemed right to get married. I took home some hairdressing products for her to use but instead of lightening her hair, it turned it pink. My mother rushed out to buy her a hat to hide her strangely coloured hair but Mum said she had to leave the price tag on so that we could take it back to the shop next day and get her money back. When we got to Martha Street Registry Office, however, the hat blew off in the wind and landed in a puddle so we were lumbered with it.

When somebody asked me later if we'd had any wedding pictures taken, as a joke I said, 'Yes, we went to a booth and got two each.'

There was, of course, no question of a honeymoon. I was back at work the next day.

We did have a sort-of celebratory night out not long after, however. We went to a club in Glasgow called Gi Gi's, but within ten minutes of checking our coats in, I shuddered and said to Kate, 'Something bad is going to happen, we need to leave now.' I don't think she had given that much credence to my premonitions up until then but she did thereafter. We had hardly gone up the road when a man was stabbed to death at the door. I feel that since childhood I have been able to sense violence before it happens. I still get these feelings of impending danger and, believe me, they have saved me on a number of occasions.

Such feelings, I have learned, are not to be confused with fear. Fear itself (and I deal with this more fully in Chapter 8) can be a killer. When not dealt with, it causes stress and stress causes physical illnesses of many descriptions, including cancer. To face fear you must first identify it and admit that it exists or else it will cause you to be depressed.

Perhaps the most common fear is of losing someone and then the natural inclination is to smother that person with love and kindness: 'I don't want you to go so here is this, this and this,' and the actual effect of that is usually to drive the other person away.

Most people don't like being disliked, so they develop different personas for different aspects of their life. Very dangerous. Like the shifting plates under the earth and oceans that cause earthquakes and tsunamis, sooner or later these facades will crash. So the moral of that is that if someone doesn't like you that's their problem as long as you are doing nothing to cause it (if you are, then change it!). We can never be comfortable living in disguise, it's false and it's horrible and it is the result of being fearful about your own identity.

In my one-to-ones with people I urge them to relax because that is the first stage to finding one's self and it's often the advice contained in messages I deliver from the Spirits. Relaxation does not mean just resting the body, it means resting the mind and the best way to do that is to meditate.

How do I do that? Many ask. Well, start by noticing your surroundings. If you are in the room, be in that room in your head, bring everything to your fingertips. If you are having a cup of coffee don't just hold the cup and think, *How am I going to get through the next week?* The next week will take care of itself if you take care of today, of the moment. Look at that coffee and enjoy it.

People who go into therapy are often given simple tasks like drawing or basket weaving. This is to focus the mind, to distract it from what might or might not happen elsewhere or in the future. To erase fear is to start getting back control of a life that could be drowned by it.

*****

FEAR comes a close second to grief in the suffering I see around the world. And here's a word of caution about the latter: Never let anyone use grief as a weapon against you. When somebody loses someone they become the centre of attention, everybody is fussing around them. A woman who has always been regarded as a wife and mother is suddenly a widow so it's natural for the family to spend more time with her, be more caring towards her. But that can't go on for ever and when that extra love and attention are reduced, the widow (or the widower) quite often demands its return. Watch out for that little bit of emotional blackmail: 'It's all right for you, you've still got a husband/wife/mother/father …'

But using grief as a weapon is bad behaviour. The family – and indeed the bereaved – have to get on with their lives.

3

Making Their Presence Felt

TOWARDS the end of the eighties, the whole mediumship thing started to explode for me and – unlike in my spiritually barren teens – I had many, many psychic experiences that were more personal to me than people I had begun getting messages for. One that stands out in my memory is the equivalent of what's known in religious circles as Toronto Blessings. That involves getting blasted with white light after someone has touched your head, but in my case no-one had touched me.

It happened as I was sitting in the Spiritual church run by Mrs Primrose, who had taken me under her wing ever since my first visit to it following the Christine Peebles episode described in Chapter 1. Despite the fact that my eyes were closed, I remember seeing this man standing in front of me – he looked oriental – and I thought, *Who the hell are you?* Of one thing I was certain – this was no dream, this was real. And then he spoke just eight words: 'Prepare yourself for the coming of the one.'

There was what I can only describe as a pulse above my head and it shot down through me like pure white light. To this day I find it hard to put into words exactly what that felt like. The closest I can come to describe it is that it felt like

I was being cleansed from head to foot and then back up again. People around me were asking what had happened to me because what they saw was me hurtling backwards – on to a seat, fortunately.

It was like a joy I have never experienced before or since other than at that very physical moment of Paul's birth. It swept away all my doubts, it was like something telling me I was connected to something far, far bigger than me. I still can't say what that is – God, Spirits, a Higher Power – it defies definition. What I am sure of is that that moment was a very defining one in my spiritual development, although there were others to come, as we shall see. Now I was certain that not only was there something greater than me out there but it had sent me a message. I had a purpose to fulfil.

I experienced a feeling of immense joy in the wake of this experience. I only had to think about it for a moment thereafter and my mind was right back in that joyous space, and that went on for weeks. It was absolute enlightenment.

When I told Mrs Primrose she said, 'Son, you are going through some change or other. Don't over-react to it; just make a note of it,' which I did. From that point on I kept a diary recording every unusual thing I experienced, which is why I am able to recount many of them accurately here. One entry reminds me of the time a monk appeared in my bedroom. I had turned in early and Kate was still downstairs when this apparition occurred. Now I am not a Christian but there he was, a monk, and when he put his hands out to me they were covered in blood. If anyone has an explanation for that, I would be delighted to hear it.

Another time I was sitting in an armchair in the sitting room when the chair started to move. Rocking backwards and forwards and then sideways, it threw me about like a bucking bronco. *Oh my God*, I thought, *what's happening now?* What did then happen was tremendous: I had my first out-of-body experience. The room seemed to be bathed in yellow light and I could see my physical body from another part of the room. For some reason Sandra, a junior at the salon, came into my thoughts and the next thing I knew I was in Sandra's bedroom – a place, I assure you, that I had never been and never have since.

I saw Sandra seated cross-legged in a basket chair in the corner of her room reading a book. It seemed like only a matter of seconds later that I was back in my own sitting room but I must have been out of my body for longer than that because it was stone cold when I returned to it, like a dead body. I got up – with some difficulty – and had to slap myself and massage my legs to get back any semblance of feeling.

At work the following day I asked Sandra if she had a basket chair in her bedroom and she said, 'Yes, why do you want to know?' Ignoring the question, I went on: 'And were you sitting in it reading a book at about nine o'clock last night?'

'Yeah,' she said, 'but that's creepy that you would know that. Were you watching me?' It has to be said that I was as baffled as Sandra. I did not go on to tell her that at the same time I had seen a butterfly fly right through me and I could *feel* every colour, every speck of that creature. It was part of me and I was part of it. Altogether a most beautiful experience but to Sandra and most people it would have sounded bizarre, to put it mildly!

*****

I DIDN'T tell Kate too much about such experiences. I was aware that she thought something was competing with her for a big place in my life.

Our second son, Steven, was born on 9th October 1984 and things were moving along nicely in our life. Steven was the most beautiful baby, with blond hair and blue eyes. It seemed for a time that everything in our life was complete. We had moved from our flat in east Glasgow to Cumbernauld because we wanted to raise our boys in a house and by now we were both doing reasonably well (Kate had a job in a shop and I was managing a hairdressing salon).

It was a bad move for two reasons – (a) We missed our lives in the bustling city and (b) There was a recession, which meant that we lost every penny we put into the house. It was a strange thing moving away from Glasgow in that it left us both with loads of time on our hands and there was nothing to do in this very drab town that we'd switched to. But there was an even more serious underlying reason: I came to realize that I was gay.

Doing a great deal of spiritual development as well as meditation at the time, I was forced to look at myself and the different issues in my life and one of the most serious things that I had hidden – even from myself – was my sexuality. I had hidden it well but now I could no longer do so. I would sit in a meditation group and realize that I could not go on indefinitely living a lie. In that setting feelings of a gay nature were constantly arising.

It is a very human thing for people not to want to look when things get too much. We bury it in the dark rooms of our minds. But however hard we fight to keep these things from coming back to the forefront of our minds, they will haunt us regardless. At some point we simply have to face up to such problems, however black they may seem. You have to lighten the load, get rid of the heavy baggage that is holding you back. By now I had learned the theory and I had to put it into practice.

It wasn't just telling Kate that had held me back from accepting the truth: there were so many other people to consider – my parents and brothers and sisters, my two young sons and many friends. As it turned out, practically no-one was surprised; so much for thinking I had been keeping a secret all these years! Besides, it wasn't fair to live a lie – not to me, not to Kate.

Kate and I were arguing a lot, but then we always did. Anyway, the arguments got worse and I had used up all the excuses for drifting away from her. When the time came, Kate just did not want to accept that I was not the sort of man she thought I was and looked for alternative excuses. It was my new friends in the Spiritualist movement, she concluded. She had never been too pleased with my increasing commitment to Spiritualism but I think she could have faced that far more easily than accept that I was gay.

In the end I didn't have to break the marriage up; it just dissolved. For a while I went back to the family's roots in the Gorbels (my mother and father had already returned there) and occupied Sammy's flat. I drove out every day to see Paul and Steven but by now there was cold anger between Kate and me. It was easily the most painful period of either of our lives.

*****

IT was a transition in life in more ways than one. I saw the meditation I was doing as part of my development to become a medium, as a self-assessment process. I had to look back and see who I was and decide whether I was happy with that person. Face my own demons, if you like; find out what was real and what was fantasy. We are all very good at putting things into the dark rooms of our minds, lying to the world, but I had to shine light into those corners and become really honest.

It was pointed out to me that I would never be able to discern what was going on in the Spirit world until I knew who I was.

The result of all this soul-searching was that I became pious (a friend calls it my Jesus period!). I gave up smoking and drinking. In my efforts to become a truly spiritual person I fooled myself into believing that I had to be utterly good and that meant denying myself all forms of pleasure. That, I believed, was what people deserved if I was to use my Gift to help them. Looking back I can see that that was ego taking over, I was making out that the messenger was as important as the message. It was some time before I learned that you don't have to be a saint to help people.

*****

ONE experience I had quite early on which really shocked me happened at a small Spiritualist church on the west coast of Scotland. I was giving a message to a woman from her husband. Everything was spot-on – I gave her his name, the date of his death, how he died and various other pieces of information. And then he said something I couldn't understand: it was the Shakespearian quote, 'Alas: poor Yorick! I knew him, Horatio.' Now I got the distinct impression that these two were very well-educated but I had never been given a piece of a great literary work to pass on before.

The woman thanked me effusively and told me I had made her very happy. After the service she came up to me and said I had told her that she was going to die soon and be with her husband. 'Oh no, I don't think so,' I said. 'That's not what I said at all.'

'Yes, you did,' she said – 'that was our code.' Whichever one died first would try and come through and recite that quotation from Hamlet when the other one's end was near. Despite her reassurances, I felt awful. 'I would never tell anyone they were going to die,' I said. 'But you didn't,' she said. 'You merely gave me seven words from the Bard. You weren't to know it was code or what it would mean to me. Take it from me, though, it was the best bit of news you could have given me.'

*****

MEANWHILE at work, John, my boss at City Barbers, did not know what to make of me. He had just started the business and, since I had a reputation of being a good barber, he brought me in to help manage the operation. Then I would say, 'John, I need a long weekend this weekend. I've got to go to Spain for a psychic event,' and he would look at me quizzically and say, 'Okay, but how does this mediumship thing work?'

John was an atheist and a hardened sceptic but he occasionally came along to see the sort of thing I did out of work hours. His desk was next to my cutting station and he kept a keen eye on me. One day he was doing the books and I was attending to a customer when the man, a sales rep passing through Glasgow for the first time, suddenly said, 'Oh, my God, it's my father's anniversary [of his death, it turned out], I need to phone my mother.' I said, 'Raymond, do you really think your father will mind?' His jaw dropped: 'How do you know my name?' he demanded. *How,* I thought, *do I get out of this?* I did my best to flannel him: 'Oh, it's just a hairdresser's knack. We get good at guessing things like people's names.' But he wasn't having any: 'I haven't mentioned my name, how did you know it?'

He wouldn't leave the shop without an answer, so John came across and asked me, 'Why did you call this gentleman by his name when you've never met him before?' I said, 'I don't know, just get him out of the shop.' He did but later he came to me and said, 'You told me this stuff never came to you when you are working here.' 'I know,' I said, 'but I'm tired and that makes me vulnerable. I can't hold it back when I'm running low.'

It wasn't long after that John witnessed another similar episode. I was cutting a gent's hair and asked him, 'Was it busy on the wards today?' He looked bemused and replied, 'I didn't tell you I was a doctor; I've never been in this shop before, so how did you know?' I said the first thing that came into my head: 'Oh, you smell like a doctor.' He gave me one of those disbelieving glances but did not pursue it.

The look I got from John, however, was different. He was beginning to think, 'There's something to this.' And I'm sure he was wondering if he could bottle and market it.

4

Doing It For Myself

I HAVE lost count of the number of times that people have asked me if I can give them Saturday's successful lottery numbers or the winner of tomorrow's race in the 2.30 at Newton Abbot. That is not what I do. I am a medium who is able to help people overcome their grief by contacting loved ones on the Other Side and delivering messages (wrapped in proof) which help them to understand that there is life beyond this one and they will be reunited.

Having said that, I cannot deny that being psychic means I do get premonitions and these quite often produce results of a varying nature. Most people dream things which have a bearing on something that happens subsequently. That's the nature of dreams, they recycle all your mental rubbish which is why they are usually confused and hard for the layman to interpret.

In America recently I dreamt that my neighbour in Scotland was selling his house and a black Audi convertible figured in the dream somehow. I phoned home the next day and found out the neighbour had put his house on the market; and when I got back there was trouble with my new car and the dealer offered to swap it for a black Audi convertible, which I accepted. Who's to know where that comes from? There is nothing you can do about synchronicity so why bother trying to work it out? Things are not always what they seem.

I remember once dreaming that Lennox Lewis was going to be the world heavyweight boxing champion before the year was out. Now, at the time, Lennox Lewis was finished. He'd started his career as a young man, he never really got very far and it was just about over for him so it was improbable to say the least. John, my boss, was a real boxing fan and one who would gamble on almost anything. So when the next day I told him I had had a dream about boxing and asked, 'Would it be possible for Lennox Lewis to get the world title before this year ends?' his reply was, 'Don't be stupid, I used to have faith in what you do, but that is just crazy stuff.' Sure enough, however, before the year ended they gave Lennox Lewis the belt – by default.

John was amazed and promptly invited me to accompany him to the Chevalier Casino in Glasgow's appropriately named Hope Street and, once inside, asked me if I could win him some money. He was an absolute atheist but he'd managed to summon up enough belief to respect me that night in the hope I could fill his pockets. I'd never seen a roulette table before but he led me to one and asked me if I could tell him on which number the ball was going to land. I said, 'No,' but he was persistent. He said, 'Look at the table and tell me whether it's going to land in the first twelve, the second or the third.' I said the middle one and to my dismay he shoved a pile of chips on it. It won and I got a feeling about the third twelve so he moved his new mountain of chips there and that won too. To cut a long story short he had three successive wins. I don't know what the value of the chips was but I guess he must have won a few hundred pounds.

I had this feeling in my gut and I said, 'John, I don't think I should be doing this.' He said, 'Why not? Let's go for a drink.' At the bar he gave me a stack of chips but I didn't know what to do with them; I shoved them all on one number and it came up. John – he's dead now, I took his funeral last year – went to a table without me and lost everything and went home full of remorse. I stayed, had a steak dinner and still went home with a bulging wallet.

*****

A LOT of people become fixated by a certain event in their lives and want to know the outcome of it; but if it's not a good outcome, it's not good for them to know. Anyway, I don't often know it and if by linking with a relative of theirs in the Spirit world I don't get an answer, I assume they have not to know. In any event even if I could do it I would not tell people what I saw in their future unless it was to help them by, say, passing on a health warning in time for them to get a medical check. To do that would mean taking away their life's experiences. Can you imagine living a life where you just knew what was going to happen? It would be Groundhog Day every day. So even if it were a favourable outcome a lot of the essence would be lost if I could and did relay such information, so I try not to do it.

I don't get a lot of bad news from the Other Side. Much depends on the condition of the person I am delivering to. I've been in a pub some nights having a drink, having a laugh and seeing something that's out of sync, that's not good.

But I would never go and tell the person. I might see a shadow, for example, that would tell me that a person was unwell or a foreboding of something bad being about to happen which has later proved correct, but unless I was in full control of my faculties (i.e. not drinking) I would not give people unsolicited messages in such circumstances.

Premonitions can be frustrating things when there is nothing you can do about them. In a dream I once saw a plane falling out of the sky into water. The plane was full of camels and as it hit the sea thousands of Arabic coins covered the surface. When I woke the following morning it was to hear that an Egyptian airliner had crashed into the Mediterranean. My dream was clearly prophetic but even if I had had it a night or two earlier, whom could I have told and what would they have done?

Even when you are able to warn someone in time, the chances are they will take little notice. Once – and this is some time before I became a medium – I had a very bad feeling about a car belonging to a hairdresser I was working with called Anne Marie. I passed it on and said, 'Don't drive that car – there's something wrong with it.'

'Nonsense,' she said. 'I've just got it back from the garage. Maybe that's what you're picking up.' Anyway, she was on her way home that night when a wheel came off as she was crossing a bridge and the car was only saved from falling into the river below by a crash barrier. She was convinced and promptly asked me to give her a reading.

*****

IT was at Mrs Primrose's church on West Princess Street that, on an autumn evening in 1990, I met Jim McManus, a softly-spoken true gentleman who is now my partner. Once Kate and I had separated and (hopefully) cleared the wreckage of our past, I threw myself into my Spiritualist activity, which involved attending meditations – that's a group activity where people go to learn just how to meditate, relax and perhaps be put in touch with a medium.

Jim's father had died more than six months earlier and he had wandered into the church hoping he might get a message from him but that was not what it was about that night. However, he started to attend regularly and I remember thinking he was a nice person. One of the people there suggested I do a sitting for him at some point but initially I said I couldn't be bothered. I had my own life to sort out. I had gone into business with my first salon at Della-Corte's (part of an Italian family's shop) and had my development to get on with so, selfishly on reflection, the last thing I wanted to get involved with was helping other individuals.

Jim was grieving the death of his father when I first got to know him, and even though he made no mention of wanting a private sitting with me a strange episode happened that meant that he never had to ask.

One evening we were chatting in his flat and I remember his father coming through to me saying, 'He's got my jacket in his wardrobe,' and I thought *Really? What colour is it?* and he replied, 'It's a tweed sports jacket.' So I said to Jim, 'You've got your father's tweed sports jacket in your wardrobe.' His reaction was an emphatic denial and he wanted to know why I was saying that. I said, 'Look, I hate to do this but I think your father wants to get a message through.' Now although both Jim's parents were Catholic they were members of a branch that was not strictly orthodox but into charismatic renewal, practised healing and the laying-on of hands – things they might not approve of at the Vatican.

A lot of bizarre things happened that night. I felt my jumper being tugged and I didn't think that Jim would notice it but he did. 'That's my dad,' he said, laughing. 'That's the sort of thing he used to do. He was always the practical joker, always playful.' I said, 'Well, watch it, he's letting me know he's going to do something else,' and with that a big rubber plant moved. I asked Jim's father, 'Did you just move that?' Jim looked incredulous: 'Are you serious?' When it moved again he said, 'Oh, my God!' He was terrified but also impressed that the Spirit could do such things if it felt so inclined.

More importantly he was delighted to get some evidence that his father had survived, evidence that would allow him to remember his father during the fun times because all he could think of up to this point, and I don't want to go into too much detail here, was that he had suffered a horrendous death that had etched itself on Jim's memory.

Nevertheless, in those early days Jim was very sceptical and asked me not to pass on any messages unless I was absolutely certain they were coming from the right source. But it has happened whether we wanted it to or not.

*****

ODD as it may seem, my foreign travels as a medium began in Torquay. Shortly after Kate and I separated I took Paul and Steven to the Devon resort for a holiday to show them that I still wanted to be part of their lives. We took out speedboats, went swimming and rock climbing – all the things that fathers and sons do on holiday. But there were naturally times when they wanted to go off and do their own thing and that left me with plenty of thinking time. *What*, I thought, *am I going to do with this medium thing? Am I going to spend the rest of my life going round these same little churches doing much the same thing, or can I widen the field, travel abroad and bring messages to people whose languages I can't even speak as Albert Best had done? Please*, I asked the Spirit world, *broaden my horizons*.

Not for the first time, my prayers were answered. When the three of us got back from the holiday there was a message waiting for me from the Gibraltar Spiritualist Society wanting me to work there and in Spain. There was also an invitation for me to do a seminar in Germany, and the Spiritualist Society of Great Britain asked me to go to Japan. Needless to say, I accepted all three.

First came Gibraltar. I had never appeared on a stage before, just church platforms. Standing backstage I peeped through the curtains and saw this vast place (vast to me at the time, anyway) packed to the gunnels with people who, for the first time, had paid to see me. *My God, what have you done?* I thought. The reply came back quick as a flash: *You asked to be here*. Then I looked through an outside window and saw a fruit tree with just one orange on it at the very end of a branch and that reminded me of something I had once been told: If you want the fruit of the tree you have to be prepared to go out on a limb.

Then I prayed again: *Please let this work*. And yet again my prayer was answered – it did.

*****

WORKING with The Gift took me into some bizarre situations. Once when I was doing my thing in Mrs Primrose's church I got a boy coming through who had hanged himself. He lived in a three-storey tenement house on a street in Possil Park on the north side of Glasgow. When I relayed this to the congregation a woman said, 'Yes, that was my son.' But another woman thrust her hand into the air and said, 'No, that was my son.' And lo and behold a third woman chimed in with, 'Excuse me, he's talking about *my* son.' It turned out that all three had lost sons while living at different times in that building and they had never met before. A pretty amazing statistic especially when you consider the fact that there were only about 40 people in the church at the time.

And as if that weren't enough the Spirits had another three-hangings experience in store for me. The accomplished medium Mary Armour and I were due at a hall in Gourock down the Clyde and on the journey there I was looking out of the car window at the cranes. Suddenly, in my mind's eye, I saw a young man hanging by his neck from one. *My God*, I thought, *what's that?* I turned my head away for a moment and when I looked back only the crane was there and I convinced myself it had been a trick of the light. But as we drove on it happened again.

I didn't say anything to anyone, but after Mary had given her demonstration and I had begun mine I got this vision again only this time there was no crane, just a man with a rope around his neck. 'There's a woman here whose son died by his own hand, he hanged himself. Who identifies with that?' A woman said simply, 'Yes,' but almost immediately another woman at the back said, 'I think you're with me.' I said, 'No, I'm definitely here. The Spirit is telling me it's this lady, but now that you've put your hand up I see another young man; you also lost a boy in this way,' and I gave them both the names of their sons. 'But the deaths were different. In the case of your son,' I said to the second woman, 'it was accidental. He'd fallen from somewhere and choked. But,' I said, addressing the first woman, 'your son was depressed and took his own life and left two children behind.' Both wept and said the information was accurate.

*****

THESE days I am no longer surprised by the amount of information that comes to me at a public demonstration. In Glasgow, for example, during my last UK tour, there were 2,000 people in the audience and every one seemed to have a question. For the benefit of those who have never attended such an event, let me give some examples of what I was able to pass on from those in the Spirit world to those who packed the Royal Concert Hall that night.

One young man who had just passed over gave me details of the locket a woman was wearing around her neck and exactly what was inside it. That allowed her to identify herself and for me to be able to tell her that he was trying to help his brother and to say that the family needed to get back together. She knew exactly what that meant but I was unable to pursue it further because a pushy Spirit came through to say she wanted her sister to know she had been with her during a skiing holiday she had just returned from.

The message and responses continued: 'She says, "I've just been skiing with *them,*" so there was a crowd of you went together.'

'Yes.'

'I am also hearing beautiful music, classical music. Does that make any sense to you?'

'Yes, she played classical piano.'

'I have a strong sense of prayer and healing around you and this is something she is telling me you are interested in. Does reiki mean anything to you?'

'I am a reiki master.'

And then her mother came through. 'She's saying something about contact lenses? Does anyone in your family have them?'

'My son wants them.'

'Right, well, she is just letting you know she's aware of it. Now she's talking about connections with Australia …'

'My cousin who's here with me, she has relations in Australia.'

'Your mother says, "You're not wearing your glasses, where are your glasses?" Now she's holding a cat in her hands. Has somebody lost a cat?'

'I've lost a cat.'

'Well, your mother's holding a cat in her hands and she says the cat is fine. I have got to mention Martha who wants to be remembered.'

'That's her sister.'

And so it went on. This woman got heaps of evidence that it was indeed her mother who was coming through.

Another woman's father came through to tell me that he had died suddenly from choking. He had something to do with ships, I told her. 'Yes,' she said, 'he was a sea captain.' When I told her that her father was remembering 'the last supper' she said that that would be the meal they had the night before he died – 'a very special occasion.' From that point on the facts flowed thick and fast and after almost every one the recipient quietly said, 'Yes.'

Another Spirit who came through said his name was John Weir. A man in the audience shouted out: 'I knew a John Weir.' I told the man that his erstwhile friend said he knew he had stopped working and the man said, 'I had to give up work.'

'Okay,' I said, 'he knows that that was something you did not do willingly. He's saying, "Don't worry," because he knows that what is happening to you is very stressful but if you can unload that stress you will enjoy the life you have. He says to think of 10th June, there's something special happening there,' to which he replied, 'That's my birthday.'

5

When In Doubt

FOR any reader who is still sceptical at this point, permit me to say that there have been moments when I doubted my own faith despite the reinforcing episodes, which I had been given again and again. Was I so good at reading body language? Was I just the world's greatest guesser? My confidence was further diminished by the knowledge that some other mediums were coming up with higher-quality evidence than I delivered – more detailed names, addresses and other information that I was often not getting. Why, I asked myself, was that happening? So, on my way to give a demonstration at the Templar Hall in Irvine in 1993, I gave the Spirit world an ultimatum: *If you don't give me something really accurate tonight, I'm packing this in. If this is something you truly want me to do, get behind me. If you do, I'll go with it. If you don't, I am just going to sit there on my backside. I will not struggle.* I felt that what I was doing carried a great responsibility and I wanted to be more than one hundred per cent certain that my messages were coming from a higher and good source and I had to put all my faith and trust in these Spirit people.

When I had been introduced I spotted a really big chap standing at the back with his arms folded, a picture of defiance. A woman called Anne Murphy came through and said she had a message for someone in the hall. At once I spotted a glow behind this man and I knew it was him. 'I believe the message from Anne Murphy is for you, sir.' 'Can't you give me any more than that?' he asked meanly. I asked Ms Murphy to oblige but for what seemed an eternity there was nothing. Then the Spirit said to me – and I repeated it – 'More? For goodness sake, I'm his bloody wife!'

Everybody laughed except Mr Murphy. His arms dropped, he was gobsmacked. So was I, but for a different reason. Everything I asked from her I then got: 'How did you die? Where had you lived?' Every time the answer was spot-on and finally, when I asked her what message she had for the suspicious widower, she shot back the answer: 'Tell him to get on with his life, he's not been looking after himself.' Again, he admitted, she was right.

I learned a lot in those few minutes: I would be given answers provided I asked questions. Up until now I had expected the Spirits to be mystical but it was all about communication.

I got a message for a woman who turned out to be a medium herself and was a little on the cocky side. It was from her mother and she said, 'Happy 50th birthday today.' 'Is it your birthday?' I asked the woman. 'Yes,' she sniffed, 'but I don't want everyone to know my age.' Her mother had died of cancer and was telling me the daughter had it too, but she would be fine. The woman narrowed her eyes and demanded, 'Have you been speaking to anyone about me?' 'Yes,' I replied, to the delight of the audience, 'but only your mother and she's on the Other Side.'

The more I animated what came through, the more I got. The tension during this demonstration was amazing, you could hear a pin drop. My senses were most definitely heightened that night. And the Spirits seemed to be enjoying it too. The answers started to come through almost before I could complete the questions.

I could have gone on indefinitely but when I finally called it a night, the medium came up to me and said, 'Is tonight the first time it's worked like this for you, son?' I tried to lie but she wouldn't have it and delivered the ultimate compliment: 'You looked as surprised up there on the platform as we were in the hall. Whatever happened, keep doing it. You have an amazing Gift.'

*****

THERE was a period when Jim's mother was dying and he wanted to take her on one last holiday but neither of us had any money. I had just started my own business at the time and was struggling with it.

Then, one evening I was at home watching *Coronation Street* when something untoward happened. Jim, who was just home from work, had gone to take a shower so I was alone when I had a vision of a spinning roulette wheel and a white ball falling into the green zero, not once but three times. I called out to Jim, 'Do you have any money?' 'A fiver,' he said, 'and a tenner I've got in reserve to buy petrol tomorrow.' 'I can't very well go into a casino with only a fiver,' I said. 'Give me the lot.' He did; he trusted me.

I went straight to the casino, bought five £1 chips and put one on the zero at the first table I came to. It lost and so did the second, so I put the remaining three chips on and won. I left the chips there and against incredible odds zero came up again. So I went to a telephone and called Jim to tell him I'd won. 'How much?' he asked. Now I'm not a gambler, so I hadn't worked out the odds, let alone counted the chips, but I knew it was several hundred pounds. 'Call it a night then,' he said. 'Don't lose what you've got.' But my instinct was to carry on. I just kept predicting numbers all over the place, winning numbers. I asked the woman what was the most I could put on a number and she looked at me as though she couldn't quite believe I was a novice. '£25,' she said; the number 8 came into my head and I bet on that – successfully. And so it went on, I couldn't lose. It was fabulous. I won two thousand pounds in an hour – all from a £5 start. And I went home with Jim's £10 petrol money still in my other pocket. The following day I found even more chips still in the blazer I'd put on just to get into the casino. Hundreds of pounds-worth more.

Jim was able to take his mother on the trip he'd been talking about just before that green zero popped into my head. They went south to visit relatives in Kent and he took her to London to see some fabulous shows in the West End. For my part I was just glad that my winnings benefited somebody else and I hadn't used my powers for my own ends. I'd have been uncomfortable with that … even if it was just luck. Who knows?

I haven't tested it again since, but others have on my behalf, so to speak. When I was coming round in hospital after an operation, I was apparently muttering things and the nurses were writing them down. When I was fully conscious they told me what had happened and what they'd done. I'd apparently told one of the nurses, 'Your mother's here,' and she started to cry. I'd given her a message from the dog she'd just lost. At that point one of the porters said, 'Get the lottery numbers from him,' and my mind started to download numbers. I never did find out whether they won. Even the surgeon asked me afterwards, 'What was all that about?' I had to tell him, 'I've no idea.'

*****

DURING my last demonstration in Washington, I was asked if I believed in eternal life. Here I was obliged to use the Buddha's view of things: there is no afterlife, just life which goes on whether it's here or in the next world. Consider existence as life in a pond. Some seeds are under the mud, some between the mud and the surface, and some have broken the surface and bloomed into a lily. It's all just a great journey that didn't start in this life and won't end in it. Our consciousness keeps expanding but because we live in a world where there are linear thought and time and space we are restricted by what we can describe and what we can understand.

The very nature of existence is about ripening our consciousness. So often people restrict themselves by thinking that everything has to be achieved or got over in this life. It is such an unburdening process to come to the realisation that there is no beginning and there is no end. Perhaps I can illustrate that by pointing to the case of a man who says, 'I hate my brother but he's family so I have to go along with him.' Why? Why would you continue on the same path as someone you don't like, someone who makes choices that contradict your own? If you dislike someone that much, take it from me, you are not going to be connected with them in the Spirit world.

I use the Bell Jar analogy, told to me by Tricia Robertson, a psychical researcher, to explain that further. The dense and heavy gas in a bell jar sits on the bottom. If someone is dense and heavy in this world, it is their mind, not their body, that is dense and heavy. So the mind will be dense and heavy in the next, and will not rise to where the gas is cleaner and lighter, any more than it would in Buddha's pond.

So what does all this mean? You don't need to hold yourself back with depression, anger or negative thoughts. Let go of them and rise to where things are so much lighter.

So yes, my answer to the Washingtonian's question was that I do believe that life is eternal. But the follow-up question was more complex: Is God punishing us when he takes a loved one from us or delivers one who is, say, disabled? No, is the short answer. When we think that way we are behaving like martyrs, like children in some respect. 'My son's not well so I'm being punished.' That's the way we often perceive life because we are frightened of it; we choose containment. To lighten up, to rise towards the top of the bell jar or the pond, we must lose the fears, the doubts, the anger, the hate. These are the things that hold us back. If somebody is killed in your family don't go down that 'What did I do to deserve this? What did I do? Why am I having such bad luck?' path. That's what we learned from birth, from our earthly parents. Just accept that your loved one died and move on. That's the way to rise to the top of the jar and live in the light. This physical life is tough and at times for some it seems too harsh — but all of our human journey is about learning.

Remember, God is not punishing you, and more times than not we grow from our tough experiences.

*****

PEOPLE find the church they end up being members of in so many different ways, but here's one that still amuses me. A woman came to our church on a regular basis. Her husband drove her there and dropped her outside before setting off to spend a couple of hours at his club. One night I gave this lady a message from her mother: 'She's telling me your husband's just won the jackpot in a fruit machine.' 'I don't think so,' she said. 'I think you'll find he has, your mother is most definite about it.'

She told me later that on the way home in the car she asked him, 'Did you win some money in a machine tonight?' and his face dropped like a stone. 'Yes,' he said, 'I won the £250 jackpot and I didn't intend to tell you but how on earth did you know?' Earth, she explained, had very little to do with it, and she told him about the message I'd given her from her mother.

He was converted. He came with her to the service every week after that!

*****

TIME and time again the words of that medium in Irvine came back to me during my British tour last spring when I had the privilege of travelling to such places as Newcastle, Leeds, Stoke-on-Trent and Leamington as well as my native Glasgow. One after the other they came at me with their questions and the Spirits didn't let me down. I think I enjoy sharing my Gift during the public demonstrations I give – whether in a small Spiritualist church or large theatre. Here are some samples of the dialogue from those demonstrations.

*****

THERE was the lady whose mother I knew had passed in January because she was telling me from the Other Side that she had been in hospital and she showed me a private room or a small ward:

'Yes, it was January of last year and it was in a small ward.'

'Her sister is there as well.'

'Yes.'

'Their names are Mary and Margaret.'

'Yes.'

'Mother is saying what a difference in the life you have now to the one you had ten years ago. You were closed off, now you have opened up.'

'That's absolutely right.'

'I see someone who has lost the sight in one eye.'

'Yes, my mother did.'

'She loved dancing.'

'Yes, she did.'

'She wouldn't get her ears pierced.'

'That's right too, she refused.'

'There's a purse belonging to her which you have.'

'Yes, I do.'

'And she's talking about someone called Frank.'

'Her brother was called Frank. He died a few years back.'

'Somebody had diabetes because she is saying, "The diabetic is here."'

'Yes, my father had diabetes and she called him "the diabetic".'

'She's saying you will remember that he wouldn't wear his false teeth.'

'That's right, he kept them in his pocket.'

*****

'I'M in touch with a man who had to be given oxygen. There are two people at his side, one is holding his hand, the other wiping his brow. His name was Joseph.'

'Yes, yes, that's for me.'

'He's saying "I love the house."'

'I'm just redecorating.'

'He was lonely at the end of his life.' – 'Yes.' – 'But he's saying he's fine now, that he's been reunited with two other men. One's name is Roy?'

'Yes.'

'He wore a cap?'

'Yes, all the time.'

'But there are two men, there's also an Albert.'

'That's my mum's brother.'

'And he's talking about 15th July, don't forget 15th July.'

'That's my son's birthday.'

'He says you go regularly to the cemetery but he says, "I'm not there, I'm here. I'm everywhere you need me to be." He died with fluid on his lungs?'

'Yes, yes.'

'He says he's wearing his "good" jacket.'

'He would say that, he was a very proud man.'

'He loved his garden and especially growing sweet peas.'

'That's exactly right.'

'I see a tree?'

'That would be the one we planted where Mum and Dad are buried.'

'There is an Anne here.'

'That's Mum's name.'

'He had problems with his hearing and he had a friend called Stan he's telling me he's met up with.'

'Right on both counts.'

*****

'I'VE got someone who died in a car accident. There were two people – a man and a woman, she died and he survived.'

'That's me.'

'You have a picture of her and every morning you talk to it.'

'I do.'

'And you can smell the essence of her in the house.'

'Yes, yes. Every time I go into her bedroom I can smell her scent.'

'She's mentioning an Abi.'

'Yes, that was her best friend at school, Abigail whom she called Abi.'

'She's shaking her head like she's showing off her hair.'

'Yes, she had beautiful blonde hair and was very proud of it.'

'She wanted a puppy?'

'Very much but we didn't have one.'

'She was called "My little princess".'

'Yes, exactly.'

'I'm getting two dates in June, the 5th and the 15th.'

'She died on the 5th, and the 15th would have been her birthday.'

'She's tinkling with a piano.'

'She did have a keyboard.'

'She wore a cap?'

'She did.'

'I see her in a pink dress.'

'Yes, she had a pink bridesmaid's dress she was very fond of.'

*****

'I WANT to speak to a Mrs Thompson. I've got a boy in his teens who seems to have been stabbed in the chest.'

'My name is Thompson and the boy I think you are talking of was killed in a motorcycle accident when he was 18 and there was a serious chest injury. He was my sister's boyfriend and yesterday was the anniversary of his death.'

'Someone had a stroke, a gentleman.'

'Yes, I knew such a man.'

'But he didn't die as a result of the stroke.'

'Correct.'

'I'm getting the number 28.'

'The 28th of this month is the anniversary.'

'He's saying "Go forward" with something.'

'Yes.'

''88–'89 is when your mind started opening up.'

'Yes.'

'I'm going somewhere between here and Birmingham.'

'I come from between here and Birmingham.'

'Now is the time to stop neglecting yourself, to take care of yourself.'

*****

'THERE'S a message for a man and woman who have an apartment in Spain. Your father/father-in-law is saying, "What's all the carry-on?" You're just about to move.'

'That's my dad.'

'Something about a wall that's in the wrong place, it's a boundary issue.'

'We're knocking down the wall of the house we're buying.'

'Somebody was in the RAF.'

'He was in the RAF.'

'He's very proud of you, very pleased with you. He likes the photograph you've just had developed. He's saying that part of him will be with you in Spain. And he's saying, "Don't worry about your grandson; I'll look after him."'

'His grandson is with him.'

'David?'

'That's his name.'

'I see a young man, I feel tired, an illness before he went. Pictures of son smiling even though he was very ill.'

'There's a motorbike for a kid.' – 'Yes.' – 'Well, he's remembered that.'

'He died on somebody else's birthday.'

'He did.'

'Re-animate the life, don't be stuck in the death. He's saying something I've never said on stage before: "We're as happy as pigs in shit."'

*****

MOST of the questions put to me are in that serious vein, but I do get the odd daft one. I frequently get asked, 'Should I marry this guy/girl?' and my stock answer is, 'Yes, if you love him/her; but if you're having to ask me the answer is probably "No."'

In Canada I was having a cigarette outside the event when an obviously intelligent woman approached me, looking terribly anxious, and said, 'Please, I need to see you. Please give me two minutes of your time.' I thought it must be serious so I told her to go ahead. She said, 'I need to know whether I should do law or medicine at university.' I said, 'What would you prefer to do?' and she said, 'Medicine,' so I said, 'Fine, then go for that.' Then she said, 'Which university should I go to, such-and-such or such-and-such?' Again I asked her which one she would prefer and when she named it I said, 'Okay then, go for that one.' She was full of fear and I guess that was coming from her parents who wanted her to do law and go to the other university.

These are issues that have nothing to do with Spiritualism and I offer my advice on the basis of common sense. Sometimes I'm a bit short, like when a young man asked me where he should live and ought he to buy a house or a flat. 'You need to see an estate agent, chum, not a medium,' I told him.

*****

I AM not proud of the incident I am about to relate here but it happened so I am going to own up to it. Jim and I and a few friends were in a pub in Glasgow watching a football match on television. Scotland were playing in a European qualifier and like every other pub in the city, the place was packed to the gills. I was very aware of a small (and well-lubricated) group of young people who were paying almost as much attention to me as they were to what was going on on the TV screen.

The remarks that I was clearly meant to hear were not flattering but I did my best to ignore them until a particularly lairy youth who was determined to goad me came closer and said in a very loud voice, ''Ere, you're that psychic barber who does all that rubbish on TV, aren't you?' His girlfriend tried to restrain him: 'Leave the guy alone,' she said. But he persisted and said (expletives deleted), 'Go on, prove it. Tell me something …'

I looked him directly in the face and said, 'You had a brother called Andrew who went to Aberdeen University but hanged himself two years ago.'

Utterly shocked, he fell back into his girlfriend's arms. The information was clearly accurate but, as I say, I am not proud of delivering it. Mrs Primrose had always told me, 'Never give messages when you've been drinking, Gordon. The spirits don't mix.'

It was a mistake and not one I am likely to repeat. But at least I was able to watch the rest of the game in peace.

*****

ONE might think that no-one would be more sceptical about communicating with the Other Side than a psychiatrist, those people who delve into the human mind in the hope of solving mental problems in others. Well, thankfully I have never had the need to consult a psychiatrist. But they have consulted me in their times of grief.

One such occasion was in Italy when I was there doing one-to-ones. A woman called Sylvia came to see me. Need I say, in view of her profession, that she was highly intelligent, as was her husband, who was also a psychiatrist and who accompanied her but remained outside the room. I became aware of a boy beside me who said his name was Roberto and that the woman seated in front of me was his mother. He had been killed in an avalanche on a school skiing trip.

Roberto delivered much evidence of his presence and his mother not only listened to it in a state of great calm, but recorded it on a machine she had brought with her. Later, after she had played the tape to her husband, he came in to see me and said (these two both spoke perfect English – exceptions on that trip), 'Mr Smith, I have listened to what you said to my wife and I have to conclude that you have never met her before – I don't see how you could have, but also I cannot see how you would know so much about our late son and what happened to him. So I must also conclude that what I heard was indeed a message from Roberto himself even though I know he is no longer alive.'

His wife, clearly overwhelmed but trained not to show it, then said that she was going to make it her life's work putting the two subjects together – the human mind and the Spirit: 'What you have done has healed me. It has helped so much that I am going to try and incorporate what you do and what I do, to find some in-between stage as a doctor and a scientist.'

I hope to hear one day that she succeeded. There are links between what we do, especially in the case of those who practice Jungian psychiatry and study the belief that we are two people – an inner person and an outer one, because this was me as a child. The whole process of my self-examination process during development was very Jungian. Whenever I speak in public I am letting my inner self come out. It is then that I am at one with myself.

*****

SHORTLY before a doctor arrived for an appointment with me back in the summer, I heard the voice of a young woman saying, 'Tell my dad I know about the baby.' I had no idea what that meant but things began to make sense when I received a call to say the doctor apologized but he was running late.

When he did walk through the door I told him, 'No need to explain, I believe you had to stay and deliver a baby.' The look of amazement on his face was a sight to behold: 'You're absolutely right.' I said, 'It was a little boy, a very difficult delivery.' Again he said, 'It was tricky, it was a Caesarean; but how did you know?'

I told him of the message I had received and that the young lady who had delivered it was here with us now. She was his daughter. She had died the previous October. She gave me a beautiful message to pass on including the information that her mother was an Italian lady but that her father was now married to a woman from Wales and that she had younger brothers who all lived in Europe. All correct, I'm pleased to say.

He cried his eyes out when she said she knew how heartbroken he had been when she died and how frustrated he was that with all his medical knowledge there was nothing he could do to save her. And she added her thanks for all he had done in her memory – some of the details in this sitting were so personal that I couldn't repeat them in this book, but the reaction of a father who has been reunited with a daughter he loved so much makes what I do worthwhile. It makes me feel so good to be able to help someone who helped so many others in his life

6

Things I Won't Do

MEDIUMSHIP often gets a bad name because of the things people who aren't proper mediums do. It has to be said that there are mediums and there are charlatans – as I shall explain.

The worst offenders are the television companies who dream up stunts to trick the gullible. One tried to rope me in earlier in the year to try, along with a bunch of other 'mediums' to contact John Lennon. I didn't consider it for a moment, knowing that the whole thing was a complete farce. I tried to explain to the producer that you can't just call up the dead. You can try, but if they don't want to come they won't. Because somebody wants you to do it doesn't mean to say it will work. There's got to be a good reason for somebody on the Other Side to come through. Why would John Lennon come through on a TV programme for a group of mediums he never knew?

Anyway, the result was that they claimed that he had written a new song to deliver for the benefit of those on this side. Can you imagine what John's Spirit would have said had it been asked to take part in such a stunt? Why on earth would he have wanted to write a song for such a purpose when he had left behind such a legacy of brilliant music?

I don't do celebrity séances. I've heard of fans hiring charlatans trying to get Elvis Presley through for them. It's an insult to his memory. I leave that stuff to the Gipsy Roses of this world.

Had Julian or Sean Lennon asked me to see if their father had a message for them or Yoko in private, I would have been prepared to try. The same goes for Lisa Marie or Priscilla Presley. But for stunts, no. The Spirits I talk to aren't dead and I don't need to conjure them up – they come to me and that's a big difference.

For similar reasons I declined when a very wealthy businessman approached me indirectly at a church in London to contact his son who had been killed in a motor accident. I was told about this by the church secretary who had been approached by one of the businessman's assistants to ask if I could accompany her to her employer's home. When told, all of my instincts told me not to do it – I had a feeling in my gut which told me that the whole thing could become very controversial and that the man wanted me to back him up on a theory he had that his son had been murdered and that it wasn't an accident. In such cases I will use my Gift to comfort the bereaved; but not to back up theories – right or wrong.

*****

LIKE any other profession or vocation, the Spiritualist world attracts its share of phonies and I feel no compunction about exposing that whenever I get the opportunity to do so. The grieving are vulnerable and deserve to be protected by those of us on a true mission. I make statements like, for example, the one I delivered to the woman about getting a connection between her and reiki (Chapter 4) and she told me she was a reiki master. I didn't ask her, I told her about the connection I was getting and a hall full of people would have known it if I was wrong. Beware the mediums who ask questions: 'And would she have done this or that?' 'Would she have died in her 70s? Well, then, she was in her 60s but looked older.' That's fishing and it has no part in what we genuine mediums do.

At another meeting I happened to attend, the hall was full of elderly women of war-generation age; the medium, or whatever he was, said: 'I can see a man in military uniform. I'm seeing a letter in an envelope. I'm getting the name George.' (A safe bet, even if nobody knew one there was a George on the throne during the last war.) Ugh!

People ask me why so many mediums have Native Americans as their Spirit guides – the beings who make the link between the Spirit and the medium. I always say there have to be a lot of Indians on the Other Side to sort out all the cowboys pretending to be mediums.

I don't need photographs, relics from the past, trances, low lighting or ectoplasm – the substance that Victorian mediums were said to exude and which supposedly shaped itself into the form of the departed. But I do usually take the sitter's hands in mine as an ice-breaker.

I once worked with a 'medium' (and I use the term loosely) who was gaining quite a reputation until he was caught out. He went around finding out as much about members of his congregation as he could. He would, for example, ask a woman, 'How long has your husband been dead?

What children do you have?' And when the time came he would go up on the platform and repeat all this stuff like he was hearing it from another place. He was a fabulous mimic and could duplicate the characteristics and mannerisms of several good mediums but he differed from them in that almost all of the information he delivered in 'messages' he had garnered beforehand.

I did eventually confront him; I had to. He and I were asked to do an event in the west country. Because it was at a social club I was most reluctant but he talked me into it on the basis that it was going to benefit a severely disabled local child. When I arrived, all my misgivings were confirmed: everybody was drinking – hardly a good environment for a demonstration of mediumship – and they also had a magician and a singer lined up for the evening's entertainment.

'I can't do this,' I told him. 'I'm not a variety act.' He got stroppy: 'Stop complaining. Just get up there and do your stuff.' Still contemplating the awful dilemma I was in, I went outside soon afterwards for a cigarette and there was our friend in the car park writing down all the vehicles' registration numbers. 'What are you doing?' I said, but I should have known. Later when he started his 'demonstration' he closed his eyes and said, 'I have a message for someone here who drives a red Rover, registration number ...' I told the organisers: 'I'm sorry but this is not working for me. You had better ask the other medium to go on again.' He was furious because I refused to take part in his 'show'. But I couldn't. It was bad, very, very bad.

Another one I knew of used to phone people he knew and tell them to come to the church because 'I'm on tonight.'

One night he even tried to deliver a message to his lawyer whom he had asked to be there. 'You, sir,' he began, 'would you understand a law firm? Why am I getting a law firm coming through?' To his credit the would-be subject was having none of it. 'What are you doing?' he said, 'I am a lawyer, you know I'm a lawyer; I'm *your* lawyer.' He didn't last too long either. He only gave two or three demonstrations because he was quickly spotted. When a medium is that accurate that fast, chances are he's cheating. I only pass on what I hear and when it's nothing, it's nothing. If it's accurate, it's accurate and the purpose of that accuracy is to put someone in touch with someone they've lost. It's not about me, not about 'Look how good *I* am.'

The fakes who set out their stall to look fantastic would never do it under proper conditions, never submit themselves to the tests others of us have and they rarely work in an area where they don't know anyone. In lectures or talks I say to my audience, 'Listen to the content of what a medium says to you. When they ask you ten things, then they're not giving you a message, they're asking you to give them information which they feed back. It's so obvious. Why would a Spirit come through just to say, "Hi, my name's Charlie." They need to have a reason they came, there's got to be some purpose to their visit, why they wanted to come through. Most of the time the charlatans are saying nice things to people like, "You know a woman in the Spirit world; well, she's here and she just wants you to know she's happy and she loves you." What does that mean? They could be talking about anybody but usually it's a figment of their imagination.'

There was this guy – I have to say this makes me laugh – who came from Liverpool and he would interrupt a message to say in his broad Scouse accent, 'Hi there, this is Jesus and in a minute I'm going to bring my mother Mary through,' and 'Mary' would come through and offer all sorts of 'information' about her son. This chap ran off with somebody's wife and as far as I know was never seen again in Spiritualist circles.

And finally there was a woman who would go into a trance, tell us she was a dolphin and flap around the stage between 'messages'. I ask you, what could a dolphin tell us unless it was the Ghandi of all dolphins?

*****

A LOT of mediums claim to have helped the police solve murders. I don't go in for that, it's not my job to solve murders but to help people get over their grief. What's more, the police don't want us to; they regard offers of such assistance as a nuisance. It would give them a bad name if people thought that all they needed to solve a crime was to call in a medium. Occasionally a publicity-seeking psychic might be told something by a friend or relative who is on the force and then report it back as evidence they picked up. You've only got to look on the Internet to find some medium's claims being repudiated by the police. 'This person is a liar, she/he never did this or that, never helped us with the case.' That's just pseudo mediums helping their careers rather than the police. I couldn't be bothered to even think of getting involved in that sort of malarkey.

I will do what I can to help any close relatives of victims who come to me. A case in point is that I gave information to the mother of a young woman who had been murdered. The information helped lead to an arrest, but the man was found 'not proven' (a Scottish legal term). More importantly, the young lady in Spirit was able to reconnect with her mother and comfort her.

Another one where I helped unwittingly was when a woman came to me from Belgium where a huge paedophile ring was operating. As soon as she sat down I felt able to say, 'You've not lost anyone.' She said, 'No, no, that's not why I'm here.' I said, 'Then I can't help you.' She handed me an envelope and by now I was feeling slightly irritable because I don't play games. However, I opened it and inside there were photographs of two children. The message I got from the Other Side was that one was buried in a shallow grave, the other beneath water but one of them would never be found. However, I was able to locate an old barn which apparently belonged to an uncle and I had a very bad feeling about the man. The police subsequently arrested him, there was a lot of child pornography in the barn, but I haven't followed the case since.

What I see is what I see and that's that. The woman never came back, apparently she'd gone to see every medium she could locate. I'm not comfortable with murder investigations. Bring me the grieving parent of a murdered child, not a detective or a bounty hunter.

The parents of one missing lad of 17 who thought he'd been murdered came to see me and I was able to tell them he had not but that he had died in an accident and his body would be found in the River Clyde. Having to give bad news is horrible, the worst thing in the world. In such a case I have to preface the message by asking, 'Can you accept it if I tell you your son is dead?' Subsequently the young man's body was found in the River Clyde and it was confirmed that the death was an accident. What helped the parents was that their son's Spirit communicated this information even before the body was found.

In Australia a magazine journalist brought along a woman to see me whose relative came through to tell me he had fallen off a cliff between Bronte and Bondi Beaches. She started to cry and said, 'You're telling me David's dead?' I thought she'd lost her husband – people assume I know these things – but it was her son who, as far as she knew, was only missing. Thankfully she phoned me a few days later to say it had helped; at least she could start to look for closure. But I felt awful.

*****

I WON'T go into the detail I sometimes get when, for example, someone died in a car wreck and the Spirit chooses to tell me more than I think the recipient needs to know. I try to move beyond that. The grieving do not need to keep revisiting the scene of their suffering. The conditions people die with are of this life; human pain is not felt in the Spirit world!

Time and time again, however, I find myself telling people that they really should face their grief if they are to move on from it. I am reminded of a story told by the late great Albert Best of something that happened to him during a mediumship visit to Africa. Albert, who was in some way related to the late George Best, incidentally, had lost his wife and three children in a fire following a bombing in Ireland and he devoted the rest of his life to helping others overcome grief through his Gift.

One morning his African host said he wanted Albert to meet a great man who had a gift of his own – he was a witch doctor. Albert resisted as hard as he could. He was very dubious about people who produced the sort of phenomena associated with what he had read about witch doctors and practitioners of voodoo. But his host insisted and Albert being Albert finally relented. He was taken to a clearing in the jungle and led to a hut where he met the witch doctor. The man who had, he was assured, been given no briefing about him looked long and hard at Albert before declaring, 'You are a man from the land of the shamrock who moved to the land of the heather where you live by a giant arena where they play sport.' Albert was impressed: he had indeed moved to Scotland after the tragedy his family suffered in Ireland, and his house overlooked Hamden Park.

But he was dubious when the man went on, 'You have been brought here today because I have a gift for you and it's a gift that the Other World says you deserve because you give so much to so many.' And with that he picked up some bones from a stool at his side and threw them on the ground. Albert said what he saw next was a cloud rising like the steam from a kettle. It was tinted and made his eyes sting. Then, in the midst of the vapour, he saw his family – his wife and three children.

As he told me the story the hair stood up on the back of my neck. I knew Albert never lied about spiritual matters. 'Wow, what an amazing experience,' I said. Albert closed his eyes and said, 'I would not wish it on my worst enemy.' We sat in silence before he continued: 'I had to let them go for a second time.'

I hadn't thought of that but my friend's face was wracked with pain.

Now with the wisdom of hindsight I would say that Albert suffered on that occasion because he had never properly dealt with his grief at the time. Instead he had submerged himself totally in the grief of others and the Spirit World was telling him it was time he dealt with it. That is why I say to people, 'Look at your pain and accept it. It won't take away the hurt but it will allow you to function and you will heal faster.' I'm sure that this experience was given to Albert for him to heal, but I feel that he didn't want to go back over the death at that time.

My schedule included a trip to Africa in August to work for ten days doing some charity work with children who are orphans of AIDS. There was never a chance of me visiting a witch doctor. However hard anyone implored me, I knew I would say no.

Albert taught me that.

*****

I GET a lot of parents, mostly mothers, it has to be said, who bring their children to me wanting to know if they are psychic. Far too often it is simply a ploy by the parent to put a tag on their child's behaviour. A lot of these kids are spoilt brats who actually need attention of a very different kind to what I have to offer. The parent who excuses outrageous behaviour on the part of the child will tell family and friends that an unseen faculty is to blame: 'Oh, it's the voices he/she hears, the visions he/she sees, the Spirit/ghost that haunts our house.' Nonsense; 99 times out of 100 the child just needs to be talked to and listened to and then set some firm boundaries.

I never encourage people to get their children to do psychic things. It never happened to me and that did not impede my subsequent progress in the psychic world. As a child I could not sit down and invoke Spirits, thank God.

True, my mother and siblings made nonsense of the things I said when the Gift began to take hold, but it did not damage me in any way so I was able to have a reasonably normal childhood if such a term could ever be applied to growing up in a house packed with people. It was absolutely necessary for me at that time to look at what was going on in my head and say, 'Am I just craving attention like they say?' Without such self-examination the belief I have today would be on far shakier ground. I was forced by the doubt of those around me to look at it, to examine how much was me and how much was influenced by external Spirit. My belief in the latter was brought about, therefore, by how certain predictions turned out to be accurate, not by the encouragement of what I would call a showbusiness mother.

A woman wrote to me recently saying she was getting a lot of complaints from the neighbours because phenomena that were going on in the house were beginning to affect them and they blamed her child who, for the past six years, had seen visions and had all sorts of disturbances going on around her.

She wanted me to see the child and I would have but to talk to her as a child, not to give her a reading – I would only have done that in an extreme case and in the company of someone like Tricia Robertson or the parapsychologist Matthew Smith, who are experts at diagnosing as opposed to practising what people like me do.

But the mother was not saying, 'My child is psychic.' She was distraught because her life was being ruined by her daughter's behaviour. And when I did offer to see her she said, 'No, I think she's fine now.' A lot of people don't want to stop it if it gains them attention; they would rather be ill than find a cure because the illness gets them attention. Rather like Munchausen's syndrome.

There can also be an element of the parent thinking, *This is the chance to become a celebrity by proxy*. I had a woman stop me in the central train station in Glasgow one day. She came running over and said, 'Hold on, stay there, don't move.' I had just come back from a tiring schedule in England and I told her I had to go and pick up my car, but she ignored all that and a lad of about sixteen appeared at her side. She said, 'This is my son,' and I replied, 'How do you do, I'm Gordon ...' but he was well primed and cut me off in mid-sentence with, 'I know who you are.' Then the mother came to the point: 'He is a medium too but he needs you to help him.'

'What do you want me to do?' I asked. 'I can point him in the direction of development groups although I don't know if they would take him at his young age.'

'No, no,' she said, 'he doesn't need any of that. He needs you to take him on tour with you, to theatres and places.'

I tried to explain that he needed to be assessed and developed if he was ever going to be a medium but people like this lady are not interested in assessment in case it turns out negative and the next step can be to discover that, instead of being truly psychic, they are mentally ill. I was willing to be tested because I thought it was right. I needed to know if what was going on in my head made sense to anybody but me.

But this woman was having none of it. She saw her son as the gifted one who did not need to go through all the hoops even when I offered the name and number of a close friend of mine who could have told her in a very short time if she was right. It turned out later that she had already taken him to see this person who had summed up the situation thus: 'Son, get back to school and stop trying to be a medium.'

The mother was furious.

*****

HAVING stated some of the things I *won't* do, let me put on record something I never intended to do. A man had contacted me on my day off from the salon to plead with me to call on him and his wife. They lived just outside Glasgow and the next day I took a train there. The man picked me up from the station and we walked to their flat. It was quite a shabby place and it was obvious they had nothing. The man explained that their 18-year-old son had been found dead on the pavement near the home he was sharing with the girl he had just married. The death had occurred only eight days previously and the terribly distraught mother, Christine, had already attempted suicide. I explained to them what would happen during the sitting and explained to them that I did not go into a trance or talk in a strange voice – but the latter was exactly what did happen.

Within minutes their son had come through and he was talking through me in a voice inexplicably similar to his and using his mannerisms, starting, 'Mum, it's me, David,' and going on to explain what had happened: he had been running home to his bride. As he was passing a particular house – and he correctly gave the gate number, he had the sensation of falling but before he hit the ground he was above it looking down on his own body. He'd had a brain haemorrhage. When he told his mother he wanted her to remember the Lake District, she said, 'Oh, that's where they had just been on their honeymoon,' and when he said, 'I am part of the brightest star in the sky,' her response was, 'That's where his father told him his grandfather had gone when he passed away.'

Other evidence poured from the Spirit and when it finally moved on and a dizziness was lifted from me, I apologized: 'Sorry, I don't normally do voices like that.' So strong was David's will to come through to his mother, that he forced his mind so close to mine that his Spirit was overshadowing me.

7

Royals, Celebs and the Crazies

I HAD heard for many years that certain members of the royal family were interested in mediums and Spiritualism. Some mediums would make such claims but they hadn't really sat for any of the royal household, although I did know one medium who truly did and this was the type of honourable medium who would never divulge the contents of their sitting.

An encounter I had was more from a distance. It took place on the afternoon of the Saturday before the Queen Mother's funeral and I was doing one-to-ones at the Spiritualist Association of Great Britain's London building in Belgrave Square. My last sitting of the day was with a woman who spoke well but had dressed down. As usual I had no idea who or what she was. I didn't need to know – I get given a number and that's it.

The woman was quite delightful and did not seem to be particularly grief-stricken. Her mother came through and gave lots of information, which she verified. Then I said to her, 'Another lady has come through and says she died very recently and that you will be attending her funeral in a few days,' and she said, 'Yes, yes, yes. Go on.' I said, 'Well, with this lady is another woman who suffered terribly at the end of her life but she's very happy now and would like her family to know that when you next call on them. I see her with a drink in one hand and a cigarette in the other because that's how you will remember her.

'Anyway, they seem to be having a grand bash on the Other Side to greet the other lady. She must have been quite somebody.' The woman smiled at me and said, 'You've really no idea who these people are or who I am, have you?' I said I hadn't and she laughed, thanked me and said she would make sure all the people I had given her messages for would get them. I was quite shocked as she said to me before she left that the funeral she was attending the following week was that of the Queen Mother. With that she smiled, said thank you and left quietly. I never did find out who she was exactly as many people of that ilk book into spiritualist places under assumed names.

There have been others like this but I must say, 'What happens at the SAGB stays at the SAGB.' After all, they are just people who have needs and it is no one's business but theirs.

There have been many people I've seen who come from the world of celebrity – most come because they are sad and need healing, but some stick in my mind as interesting as they have been given messages from the Other Side which have forced them into making changes in their lives in order to heal other situations.

One I recall was a TV presenter who wanted to know if he could contact his dead father. He got more than he bargained for when his dead father-in-law came through and told him to stop cheating on his daughter!

The man was stunned, to say the least, when the 'spirit-in-law' gave information about the whereabouts of this affair and how long it had been going on etc. Recently I read that the couple had separated and that this was due to an affair that the husband had been having that had since ended.

The mother of a TV actress came though and said, 'You're having an affair, it's been going on for three years and it's got to stop, it's got to be sorted.' She said to me, very indignantly, 'I'm not having an affair,' and I said, 'Yes, you are, your mother's here and she's telling me you are and that if you don't stop it now you're going to lose everything.' Although she was very well-known she wasn't wealthy in her own right, but her husband was. I went on: 'Your mother's saying if your husband finds out he will cut you off without a penny and remember, he's loaded. So don't lose this marriage.' Her response then was, 'Well, it's not really an affair,' and I cut her off abruptly, saying, 'That's none of my business; I don't care if you're having a dozen affairs, I'm giving you a message from your mother.' She said, 'Okay, I'll deal with it.' She did and she and her husband are still together. As she left, by the way, she looked over her shoulder, gave me a wink and said, 'I don't have any doubts about you – that's exactly what my mother would have said to me.'

*****

ONE of the most interesting celebrities I have encountered in my work was William (Bill) Roache, the actor who plays Ken Barlow in *Coronation Street*. He and I were due to speak together at the SAGB and he asked to meet me first, so when I was in Manchester for a book launch a couple of years ago we met up at the Lowry Hotel. I thought I was going to be doing a sitting – because that's the way it usually is with celebs – but as soon as he walked into the room he said, 'I don't want a sitting; I have no need of any proof of life after death, I believe in it completely. I would just like to have a chat with you. There is something on my mind and if it comes up, all well and good. But there's no pressure on you whatsoever, Gordon.'

As he said that I got a picture in my mind of a particular house and I said to him, 'Don't worry, things are going to go all right with the house.' He just smiled and said, 'That's all I wanted to know. You've no idea how much that has helped,' and we carried on our conversation. I found him a most fascinating man; his in-depth knowledge of the Spiritual world quite shook me. He had a great take on the subject and I was blown away by the sheer personality of the man. He knew a lot; he had had a great number of Spiritual experiences.

A couple of weeks later we worked together at the SAGB and the talk he gave was so impressive I was reluctant to follow him. What he had to say was so gripping. He talked about his work and his understanding of his life here and in the hereafter. It was funny, it was touching; it had everything. The man's conviction in his Spiritual belief did not conflict with any religion; he just had this amazing Spiritual knowledge that was so uplifting. Everybody who was there on that day agreed that we had listened to something very special. I've heard many great Spiritual teachers talk on their subject but Bill Roache seemed to touch on the widest aspect of the subject. His mind was so open. We were shocked because we see him as Ken Barlow – not a particularly exciting character – but it was hilarious in places. He said that for someone who was supposed to be very boring he's had a pretty active life. He'd been married three times (in character) – twice to the same woman – adopted children, witnessed so many dramatic deaths, how could anyone say that added up to boredom?

He talked about various psychic experiences he'd had, some of them when he was in the Army, which have followed him through his life. He seemed to cover everything and we were taken on the flow with him, a lovely gentle unfolding of his own Spiritual development mixed in with personal details of his life.

He said to me, 'I don't need proof from a medium; I've seen visions myself. These things happened to me so they're not up for question.' He was fascinated to know about the work that I do and why I do it and he was really pleased to learn that I did it to help others who are suffering from their grief. He said that was a great introduction to a Spiritual life.

He told me he has left his sons a beautiful letter about where his Spirit will go when he dies. It was such a lovely thing and so reassuring for his family. On his death they will get his account not only of his life but of his Spiritual journey in this life and his connection with them spiritually and where he's going on to and how he will still be able to communicate with them. It says, 'This is me, don't worry about me when I die, this is where I am spiritually although you may not recognize it.'

I plan to do something like that for Paul and Steve. I would like to think that when I've passed over I will be able to come back once for my boys so that they can say, 'Wow, everything he said was real.' A personal experience for them alone so that they can recall what I did as a person, because the mind can get in the way of that. I want them to know that I'm not dead, I've just moved on. That would allow them to get on with their lives and me to get on with my journey.

*****

ONE actress with whom I very quickly bonded was Claire Sweeney who has gone on to great things since she first came to our attention in the TV soap *Brookside*. I had been asked if I was interested in doing a television series based on mediumship. When I said, 'Yes,' they said, 'Then we'll need to find a presenter.' Now I had presented things on television and it seemed an unnecessary search, but I had learned by this stage that TV people never listen to anyone and never read anything but instead have their own ideas, so I went along with it.

My attitude changed when the TV company arranged a meeting at the Berkeley Hotel in Knightsbridge with Claire to see if we would get along. We got along superbly but after the meeting's initial purpose had been fulfilled, Claire became edgy. 'Are you wanting to go?' I said. 'Because there's nothing else for you to do here today. Be on your way.' She was very grateful and whispered in my ear that she was meeting someone for a meal – it was a chap she had met on a plane on a trip to America. They had got on very well and had become good friends.

One of those mental pictures came into my head and I gave her the name of the man in my mental picture and asked if that was who she was meeting. Her face dropped and she collapsed back in her seat. 'How on earth did you know that?' she said (though in slightly less polite terms). 'I'll tell you something even more surprising,' I said, 'He's my cousin.' Now she was truly gobsmacked. 'Don't be so stupid,' was all she could manage this time, 'How did you know I was meeting a man who turns out to be your cousin?' 'I just do,' I said. 'I've got a mental picture of you two together.'

She said she was sure he would have mentioned that he had a cousin who was psychic during their long discussion on the plane. And with that she picked up her mobile phone and called him. 'Do you have a cousin called Gordon Smith?' she demanded. 'Yes, but where are you? I'm waiting for you at Mr Chow's. Are you coming?' was the gist of his reply. With that she handed me the phone and I spoke to my cousin for the first time in many years. He was as shocked as Claire and invited me to join them. I went along just to prove to both of them that this was all happening for real. I didn't stay long. But I saw plenty of Claire thereafter.

When the pilot for that show had been filmed, Claire said her record company had laid on a private jet to take her to Glasgow and would I like to take the ride with her. I was due to go home the next day anyway, so I said I'd love to. Once the plane was airborne and we were enjoying our first glass of champagne, the pilot came back to chat. He asked if either of us would like to take his seat for a few minutes next to the co-pilot who was flying the plane. I didn't need asking twice.

Once he had briefly explained the controls to me, the co-pilot said, 'And are you a singer too?' I said no, and told him I was a medium. He wanted to know what that was but I said it was too complicated to go into there but I was able to tell him that he had recently lost his mother to cancer and that she was there at that moment with us. He was stunned. I gave him a message from her and passed on her assurance that she was happy. He was a happy flyer too that night.

*****

ONE woman I met in the course of my work – a bit of a socialite, actually – had been married to a titled man who treated her horribly. She had been a photographer and a free spirit living on the King's Road in Chelsea when he met her, got her pregnant and took total control of her life. Once they were married he would never let her go out and when he did he insisted on choosing her clothes. A total control freak and, as it turned out, a very, very mean man. When he died he'd tied up his money and left her with a pittance with which she was just able to buy a shabby flat in Devon not far from where she had once lived in captured splendour.

I duly delivered a message from her husband in which he tried to justify his actions. She showed no emotion but when the sitting was over she gave me a big smile and said, 'And now, Gordon, I'm going to take you out for supper.' Supper turned out to be fish and chips in a delightful café in Devon, which was where I was working. The fare was fine for me and clearly she preferred it to the stuffy dinners she had had to endure at opposite ends of a long dining table in the mansion she had once called home – though it was more like a prison – for so many years.

She talked to me about what it had been like to be the wife of a multi-millionaire and having to live like a scullery maid confined below stairs. Now she was free and she was obviously enjoying that freedom to the full.

At one point in the conversation I said something about how I was sorry the message had turned out to be so meaningless, but she replied, 'Oh, Gordon, don't fret about that. In fact it was perfect. Now I know he's gone. I just wanted to make sure the bastard was dead!'

For reasons of her own she had taken the phrase 'letting go' to the ultimate extreme but I cannot over-emphasize how important it is to detach once someone has passed over. I put this into practice when Jim and I were on holiday in the south of France some years ago. We were sitting on the beach in Nice on a beautifully sunny spring day when I suddenly had this awful feeling sweep over me. I said to Jim, 'We've got to go back to the hotel, something bad has happened,' and he said, 'Oh, don't start.' 'No,' I said, 'this is seriously bad.' He took one look at my face and realized I meant it. 'We've got to go back to the hotel because there's a message waiting for me and I know that somebody's died.'

We walked along in silence and I had this horrid feeling in my body. I was certain there was just such a message and I needed badly to know who it was. Could it be my father or my mother?

Sure enough when we got to reception there was a message: I had to phone home urgently. I called Paul and he apologized for bothering me on holiday but said he thought I ought to know that my Uncle Michael had passed. He was only in his early sixties and had just retired; he had died by falling off a roof. Now Michael and Sylvia (who had died of cancer a few years earlier) had been like a second father and mother to me and I was shocked. Jim and I had made plans for the day and he was about to cancel them when I said, 'Give me fifteen minutes.' I sat down in our room and sent thoughts out to Michael: 'I can't feel you at the minute but I know you are out there somewhere so I'm just going to send you thoughts, praying that you make it, that you will be with Sylvia and that you will point me in any direction so that if I can be of use you will know how to contact me. Come on now, Michael, don't hang around, leave this life and move on.' Finally, I reassured him that his little dog Jo-Jo would be fine, and then went in search of Jim to say, 'Right, now, let's go out and carry on with what we were doing.' 'Are you serious?' he asked. I assured him I was, there was nothing more I could do for Michael at that point. It was up to me to get on with my life, to let go of him.

And that night we went out. I was able to relax and enjoy myself as I had a strong sense that Michael was safe and with his loved one on the Other Side.

The following day I sensed that Jim was still surprised – to put it mildly – that I was able to get on with life so quickly after Michael's passing, so during our walk along the sea front I explained to him that if the Spirit World wanted me to do something to help someone who was still here, they would put that someone in our path. I didn't have long to wait. We strolled into a bar but Jim wanted an Irish coffee and they didn't make one so we were diverted to another hostelry, which was not one we would have chosen; it had chosen us. We took a small table on the pavement outside, were enjoying our drinks in the sunshine and having a deep and meaningful discussion about philosophy (!) when a woman walked by. She was especially noticeable because, despite the heat, she was wearing a heavy overcoat, dragging a large suitcase and looked terribly flustered. It was clear that she had been crying.

'Excuse me,' I said, 'do you need any help?' She stopped and gave me a look of deep distrust but I did my best to reassure her by waving an arm in Jim's direction and adding, 'We're together. You have nothing to fear. Take the weight off your feet and let me get you a drink.' She thought for a moment and then sat down with us. Over a cold beer she gradually got enough confidence to describe her dilemma. She was a doctor from Finland whose husband had recently left her with two children to raise, and her mother had just died. The high cost of living in her homeland had obliged her to accept some secretarial work during a conference in Nice but first her flights were mixed up and when she finally did land in the resort she'd discovered there were two hotels of the same name and she'd gone to the wrong one. As a result she had lost the job and now the trip she had taken to earn some money was going to end up costing her.

I had no intention of telling her what I did – I didn't want her to think she'd ended up with a couple of loony mediums but when she talked about her mother's death I did say I had a strong sense of her mother being around her She commented: 'Sometimes I think the same but I feel stupid calling on my mother for help when I know she is dead.' She had clearly lost her faith in her fellow human beings: her husband had deserted her, it must have seemed to her like her mother had done the same thing and none of her friends was willing to look after her children while she was at work. She needed a little miracle.

After a couple of hours with us she announced that she needed to get to the hotel where she was still booked for that and the next night. But first she had a call of nature to answer. As soon as she left for the loo, Jim said, 'Is her mother coming through to you? Can you give her a message?' 'This, Jim, is one time when someone needs practical help more than a message. Give me all the money you have on you.' Jim did not hesitate. I took the small roll of euros he handed over and stuffed them into a make-up bag she had left on top of her other bag and zipped it up. She came back, thanked us for the drinks and after I had made her promise to enjoy the next day – her last in France – with a stroll around this lovely town, she was gone.

I like to think that when she found the money secreted in her make-up bag she would think that an earth angel had come to her rescue, that a little of her faith in human nature would be restored, that it had brought a smile to that tear-stained face.

'You see, Jim,' I said, 'if we're meant to do something it will come to us. We don't have to go looking for it. I know I can't go out and heal the world but if I am patient enough I will get opportunities sent my way to do what little I can.' And with that we got up and went back to our hotel to telephone my mother who was naturally distraught about Michael's death. But I knew she wouldn't stay distraught for very long and that she would take care of what had to be taken care of. My mother and father have lost all of their siblings and have coped – not because they wanted to, but because they had to. Jim and I stayed on for the last two days of our holiday. I know that when my mother and father's times come I will be able to let go of them, too. It is so important, not just for the survivor but also for those who have passed on, to let go of them.

*****

ON a dull Saturday afternoon last May (2006), I was driven to a house in a suburb of Dublin for what proved to be as much an enlightening experience for me as it was for the person who had asked to see me. The house could have been a set from the Glastonbury Festival: everything about it was hippy, from the orange and yellow cloths that seemed to cover every item of soft furnishing to the colourful paintings on the walls. I was led into a drawing room where an unshaven figure sat at one end of the couch. This was Shane MacGowan, lead singer of The Pogues and often referred to as the Mick Jagger of Irish soul music.

Oh, my God, I thought, *what have I let myself in for here?* Looking at him, I had no idea what I had let myself in for. He was clearly not in the best of health and at first I thought he looked very ill or disturbed in some way – isn't it funny, but you should never judge a book by its cover. When Shane left the room for a moment I reminded myself that I was here to try to help him as a medium, not to judge or condemn the way he looked. I could not have been more wrong about this man – or should I say this 'poetic soul'; this turned out to be a truly memorable experience for both of us.

Since Shane had a journalist with him to write later an account of the proceedings from his viewpoint I have no compunction in relating here exactly what happened. No sooner had he sat down than lots of people came through – this was clearly a man the Spirit world wanted to communicate with. First was an uncle of his. That seemed to break Shane's heart. He just sat and sobbed as I delivered his uncle's message.

Next came two people who had meant different things to him. A relatively young man who had died a traumatic death said that his name was Charlie or something and while he had not been closely connected with Shane he wanted him to know that his own head was 'very mixed up' when he met his end on earth: 'I was absolutely screwed but all that's sorted now.' Before I got these words I told Shane that I heard a very loud bang, loud enough to shake me up, accompanied by a bright flash. I couldn't understand the relevance of that; that was a different world from the one I inhabit. I believe it was a young rock star who had taken his own life by shooting himself.

The journalist begged me to get more but there was no more. That particular Spirit had said his piece and was gone.

Next came a woman who gave a personal message and took him back to when they had been recording together. Whoever it was I found myself the piggy-in-the-middle as she asked him to remember how they had had to record their duets in separate studios because they couldn't get on. 'You were a bastard,' I told him she was saying. 'And tell her she was a bitch,' he responded.

Next came an Irish poet from the Victorian era who said he had been with him in spirit during his days in Kent. 'I was born in Kent,' said Shane, which surprised me because I regarded him as a quintessential Irishman. 'Yes, I was born in England and I hated England.'

'Nevertheless,' I said, 'this man was guiding you and you had psychic visions of him and this guy actually gave you songs, he pointed you in the direction of his poems which you have turned into songs.' This, he said, was all true.

Later the journalist told me that she had often come to the house and Shane had locked himself in the bathroom to write the very music that went with the words of the nineteenth-century Irish poet James Clarence Mangan who gave voice to Irish nationalism before and during the famine years and, ironically, was melancholic, alcoholic and almost certainly addicted to opium.

And so it went on. When I left that house I couldn't help but feel that I had got the better half of the deal from this sitting. I knew that I had met an extraordinary man for whom this world is perhaps too harsh, for he surely feels the pain of it; and when later I played some of his music I could see where the angst was coming from, the rebellion that goes on inside him, the suffering that reverberates through him.

It was a beautiful and memorable encounter.

8

Healing and Dealing With Fear

MY work as a Spiritual healer does not always require making contact with the Spirit world. A woman I know well was suffering terribly from fear (which, it should be remembered, can be anger turned inward) and she came to me asking if I could bring forward her late father so that he could apologize to her for the harsh way she reckoned he had brought her up.

I knew this woman well enough to know that her problems lay here in this world. She was in a terribly abusive marriage and I pointed this out to her unequivocally. 'Don't go blaming the dead,' I said. 'Your father never did anything to make your husband the way he is – he was a strict man but openly and honestly strict. Your husband is not; he is a sly, angry man. There's not a lot wrong with a flash of honest anger from which a person can calm down – it is, after all, a natural defence mechanism. But someone who can sit in a cold state of anger with it boiling away inside while on the surface he or she looks pleasant and speaks calmly, is psychotic. There's no other word for it. To rage internally is highly dangerous and you know that because you've suffered the rages. Your woes are on this side and you need to deal with them here.'

Mediumship embraces many things and healing is one of them. Healing is part of the work of a medium and my job in this situation was not to go to the Spirit world but to show her how damaging the fear was and then to teach her how to deal with it by using relaxation, meditation and, ultimately, confrontation. It did not require intervention from the Other Side.

I should explain here that I had listened to countless accounts of how the husband treated this woman, and not just from her but from relatives and friends who bore witness to her ongoing suffering.

A violent alcoholic, he would come and, without saying a word, start to choke her. It might later emerge that she hadn't got his evening meal ready because she too had a job and sometimes was required to work late. The guy was psychologically messed up, and very badly too.

Once she'd finally worked up the courage to leave him, I began to give her hands-on and Spiritual healing. I taught her how to breathe normally again and how to correct her posture because to look frightened is often the way to lose confidence again.

I would say, 'You're absolutely exhausted, you've not slept,' and she would ask me how I knew that because she had gone to so much trouble to try and look well even down to putting drops in her eyes to make them sparkle. But I was looking into her soul and it was clear that was not well. It was obvious that something was disconnected, something needed to be reconnected, and I did get her to do loads of physical meditation, walking meditation rather than static meditation. Walking meditation is being aware of each step you are taking, instead of doing it robotic style as most of us do most of the time. It's just like a computer: you think, 'I will go from here to there,' and that's what your body then does for you.

So to distract her from the fear I got her to think about each step, lifting each foot slowly and putting it down to make contact with the ground again before lifting the other. That's the first thing I did – taught her to walk by thinking. It works wonders, I promise. That done indoors we started to go out for walks and pay attention to where she was stepping, noting blades of grass, flowers, weeds, whatever, in the small area around each of her feet. It focuses the mind, it brings us into the here and now; it's healing. This is a practice in mindfulness – to help people to connect to the here and now in a very grounded way, which stops them from living in their head, full of thoughts of fear and dread.

It took a while to restore her confidence but when it did come back it was a joy to behold. I would recommend anyone who suffers as she did to face the fear because when you are too frightened to do so you become separated from reality and simply end up where you feel safest – in no man's land. And that's a bad place to be. You convince yourself that nobody can see you, but everybody sees you. Talk to somebody about your fears. It makes it so much easier to get well.

People with a plight like hers make excuses. 'He's basically a good man; a lot of it was me, my fault. I have to admit it. I never had his dinner ready in time; I never did this, I never did that.' Rubbish! That was the conditioning she had become used to. She took the blame because it had been heaped on her for so long.

Some days I could see the danger of her slipping back into her old thinking. 'Don't quit,' I would tell her, 'just before the miracle happens.' And it did. One brave day she gave him back the blame. She didn't do it at home where he would have beaten her up yet again. She went to work knowing that there he would be sober (or relatively so) and in front of those who saw only his pleasant face. And there she gave him back the hell he had for so long given her: 'You're the bastard who has been holding my life back, beating me into submission time and time again. You're not a nice man, you're a horrible bully.' And in the few seconds it took to deliver the message, the silence in which he had conducted this side of his life was shattered. She got back her power and he became like a lamb.

Like I say, she left him and he vanished – from the area, at least. I have been asked by those who were aware of my work with this woman what I would have done if the husband had come to me for healing. The answer is there was nothing I could have done for him. He needed to confront his own demons and from what I knew of him he was unlikely ever to do that.

*****

FEAR was something I carried all my life until I did my development. I was particularly fearful of violence and confrontation – I had seen too much of them, growing up where I did. When I think of my young life, all I wanted was for people to get on with each other; my way of thinking was to get on with life and not to cause people to become argumentative or aggressive.

Throughout my teens I would look at guys and think, 'He looks aggressive, I'm nervous of him.' That doesn't happen today. In order to practise as a medium I have had to learn how to overcome fears of self-doubt and loss.

The faith brought about by my belief takes me beyond fear, beyond death even. It's very comforting to know that fear and faith cannot live in the same heart. What most people fear more than anything is that there is no life after death, that they will simply not exist once their remains have been laid to rest. And that's where I come in.

*****

AS a medium I have to think, *Okay, what if someone I love dies, what can I do about it?* And the simple answer is, nothing. I had to take a close look at that. So many people will not look at death, at the death of a loved one especially. That's something I have done; at first I dreaded doing it, but now that I have, that fear has gone away. I have to contemplate various painful scenarios which I hope will never come to pass. Again and again I have had to examine the question, *What will I do if one of my children dies?* Instead of tucking it away we have to look at things like that because it can happen and for so many people I have sat for as a medium it has happened.

Thankfully I do not have the problems experienced by Rita of Sussex who came to see me early in the summer. By the grace of God, my boys are not into drugs, but Rita's son Joseph became an easy target for pushers when his father died while Joseph was still in his teens. I didn't know any of that, of course, at the start of the sitting. I was aware that Rita must have heard the laughter from inside the room as I told the previous message recipient that her mother was sending thanks for granting her wish to have Gracie Fields's recording of *Wish Me Luck As You Wave Me Goodbye* played at her funeral.

But there was no laughter emanating from Rita, an attractive middle-aged woman, just a face etched with pain. She could have lost anybody, her parents, her husband, a child of either gender. I closed my eyes and saw several silhouettes but, I told her, the main one was of a young man, probably in his late twenties when he died. I started to get a feel of his character; I said he was very depressed at the end of his life but he was also very angry: 'You and he fell out before he passed.' She nodded.

I said, 'This boy died from a drugs overdose or something like that but it was accidental, he did not commit suicide, he's taken heroin or something like that which was either lethally mixed with something or else it was too pure.' He then told me that his name was Joseph but they called him Joe. His mum wanted to know if he was with anyone, and I said I would ask.

'There's a sister of yours in the Spirit world called Emma and she died fairly recently – after Joseph.'

'Yes,' she said, 'that's correct.'

'But Joseph's also talking about having a father there.'

'Yes,' she said, 'his father died of a massive heart attack more than a dozen years ago.'

'Your husband says he was very angry with you and very mean to you and he wants to apologize and your son wants to say sorry too for what his habit put you through.' Rita bit her lip.

And then her husband said the strangest thing: 'You've found the happiness that you deserve and I'm pleased you've found a man you really love.' And Rita smiled and said, 'Yes I have. Thank you.'

'That goes for both of them,' I added, 'because they say they knew you felt guilty.'

Then another sister, Nicola, came through for her and she was followed by several others because it works so well for someone who has as much grief as Rita had in her life. And then Joseph said he was looking after a little girl and his mother said, 'That'll be his daughter.'

Finally, he was saying he died on his own in his home after a group of people he'd gone off with – against her wishes – left him, and Rita confirmed that his body was found in a flat where several people had been living. She was delighted to know that he had not committed suicide because despite an open verdict she had always suspected that he had

'There is a lovely Spiritual energy around you,' I was able to tell her before she left. 'With what you've been through you can't help but be more compassionate about things. You have seen Spirit lights; just acknowledge them. They're waiting for you to bring them forward, to take up the reins and say, "I'm ready to use this power now." The Spiritual energy around you is very powerful. When you see blue light, remember, it is a strong healing energy and it is for you.'

*****

WHEN I am delivering a deep and personal message to someone who is grieving, I sometimes have to work hard on myself not to show my own emotions. Part of the discipline instilled in me during my development was about not becoming immersed in the emotion of what I am doing.

It's like being an emotional lifeguard. There's no point in throwing yourself into the emotional sea engulfing those one seeks to help because there's a danger of drowning with them. You have to stand on the side and pull them out.

Nevertheless I am only human. At times I have felt helpless, and, yes, there have been occasions during one-to-ones (I have never let it happen during a public demonstration) when the tears have flowed freely from me, particularly when I sense the emotion coming from the person on the Other Side – like when I have been able to bring a husband and wife together, for example. That can happen particularly when an amazing message is coming through and I have to tell the recipient: 'I'm fine, don't worry, it's not me, it's just a feeling.' And there's me with tears just running down my face! The emotions just overflow but they are not mine. All the while I am trying to disassociate myself from the message or else I'm in danger of becoming too gushy. It always amazes me how much emotion builds up during a private sitting, especially when the contact in the Spirit world has been a loving partner coming through to convey his/her love for the other – there are occasions when I feel like an intruder.

There are even occasions when I say something to someone and I don't believe what I'm saying, but I can't stop it. I would be interfering with the message if I allowed any doubts I may have to get in the way. It could be that I am saying something like: 'Your child is growing up in the Spirit world,' and I'm thinking, *Don't be so stupid, that can't happen.* But that's what the sender needs the recipient to hear at that particular time and I am not allowed to interfere because that's what they need for that stage of their grief, and how I see things on the Other Side may not be relevant or helpful to someone who has no prior knowledge of the subject.

What you try to do is give that person what they need to bolster them, to give them back some form of normality so that they can start to accept the situation. As they grow emotionally, then the Spirit moves away from them, and that's healthy. Otherwise they will form neurotic attachments to Spirits and unseen people, which is unhealthy. Once the Spirit has made the first contact with them, hopefully their mind will start to develop an understanding of linking to the Spirit loved one through their own thoughts, and they will see them as alive in an unseen world, as it were.

But no, I don't usually get overly emotional with things if I can help it. Sometimes during conversations with people afterwards when I see how dire their situation is, and I feel for them. But that's when I'm thinking personally, not as a medium. It allows me to count my blessings and think how glad I am that I am not that person. In a sense there is a great reward in seeing that you are not emotionally crippled like the person you've just seen.

*****

I AM often asked how long it is, after a person has passed over, before he or she is able to make contact from the Spirit world. It varies with the person. In some cases it is years of our time (none of theirs, remember; there is no such thing as time on the Other Side) and in others it can be remarkably quickly. I was giving a demonstration one night when I said that I saw a man in a uniform with an Alsatian dog, clearly a guard dog, and I named the street he lived on. Did anyone identify with that?

'Yes,' said a woman at the back. 'I know who you are talking about.'

After giving her various items of evidence, I said: 'He fell asleep and he was gone. A very natural death.'

'No,' she said. 'Everything else you've said about him is correct including his first name. But he's not dead.'

I tried to end the session because it was getting uncomfortable. Finally I said, 'Are you able to look in on him on your way home tonight?'

'I can do better than that,' she said. 'We live at the same address. I'm his wife.'

I felt awful because I suspected what lay ahead. She sent her brother to the church the next day to get a message to me: she had gone home after the meeting and was unable to get into the house. The police were called and they kicked the door in and found her husband lying dead on the couch. That was weird. After all, I was there that night to help people suffering with grief and she had not even started the grieving process. On reflection, she probably thought I had had a premonition, but it wasn't just a premonition. The man was dead and I knew it.

*****

THERE are times when I am reminded that I am not in control, when what I do will not work however hard I try. There was just such an occasion in a Spiritualist church in Glasgow where I was scheduled for the platform on two consecutive nights. On the Sunday the place was packed and everything went well, Spirits came through and the messages were abundant. There was nothing to suggest what was going to happen the following night. I felt equally good but nothing came through. I stood there in silence. The president of the church said, 'Shall we play some music? A hymn perhaps?' but I apologized and said, 'It's just not going to work.' At that moment I wanted to run away. I felt like a comedian facing an audience without a joke or a funny thought in his head. Imagine that if you will.

Luckily for me, in the front row was an elderly medium called May and I asked her if she would take over. She did and she was fabulous so there was nothing wrong with the room that night. But for whatever reason I was Gordon Smith Unplugged. It has happened on several occasions over the years. I have even been in the middle of something and it has just stopped and I've had to say, 'Sorry, people, it's finished.' I talked about this with Albert Best and he said it had happened to him many times during the course of his mediumship. 'There's nothing you can do, son,' he said.

Now that I am growing in confidence I can chat with an audience and tell them of things spiritual that have happened in the past; but ever mindful of a power greater than me controlling what is going on, I don't fight for what isn't there.

*****

IT was Albert who introduced me to Kathy. He had been giving her Spiritual healing but found himself too unwell to resume the work when she was diagnosed with cancer. My only purpose was to deliver the healing but the very first time she came to me I picked up a number of people around her from the Spirit World. I got a sense that all these people – including her mother – were really close to us and after a few minutes' consideration decided to tell her so.

Kathy was puzzled. 'Why is that?' she asked. 'Why are you telling me that?' I explained to her that in addition to being a Spiritual healer I was also a medium. 'And they really are here?' she asked. 'Well, you and I have never met before and I can tell you that in addition to your mother, your father is here and your sisters.' I then proceeded to give her the names they were giving me and details of how and when they passed over.

At this point Kathy turned to me and said, 'I am going to get well, aren't I?' The only answer I felt able to give to that was that she should get that information from the doctor and the hospital who were treating her cancer. My job was to give Spiritual healing.

When she came back the following week I sensed a remarkable improvement in her condition. It was an amazing turnaround yet the Spirits were still there in abundance and I told her so. In stark contrast, in the third week I detected a considerable deterioration and it was obvious that she was far from well. Then she asked me if the Spirits were still there and when I said they were she said, 'I wonder if they are there because they're preparing for me to die?'

I didn't answer but left it for her to draw her own conclusion; but the Spirits seemed in even closer proximity and I had to wonder if the healing I was delivering was to help her get well or to prepare her for a peaceful end. It was interesting, though, that when she first came to me she had no belief in the afterlife but in this short time she seemed to have acquired one.

She died within a week of that third session but I am happy to report that before that happened she took my advice and contacted the son from whom she had been estranged for years and he came over from his home in Jersey to make it up with her.

I remember Kathy especially because I had never experienced anything quite like this before. The first time she came I had given her these very accurate messages from the Spirits who came through; the second time I could actually *feel* their presence and the third time there was a bright light in the room. I didn't know whether they were coming closer to her or whether she was on her way to meet them. All I knew was that I was in the middle.

Something was preparing her for what was to come because on that third occasion her emotions were unlocked and she unburdened herself to me. As a result of that she was able to make peace with her son.

Now shortly afterwards there was an interesting sequel to this. The house where I gave Kathy her healing was the home of a mutual friend of hers and Albert's, a lovely elderly lady called Agnes. During my visits I had also given Agnes healing and messages, just as Albert had done over a number of years. She was a very spiritual woman.

One night I was sitting in a private meditation circle at a church with a number of people I was close to including Dronma, who is a psychic artist with strong Buddhist beliefs and an astonishing gift. A psychic artist is someone who is able to draw the person who is coming through to a medium and during all the times we have worked together she has reproduced likenesses with great accuracy.

Suddenly all six of us came out of our deep state of silent meditation and I announced that I knew someone was about to ring the doorbell. That happened but when you are in such a circle you cannot break it and we just had to sit quietly until the person stopped ringing the bell and went away.

Then when we resumed our meditation Agnes came through to me. At that moment Dronma began to draw and I said, 'Agnes has died.' Dronma showed me her drawing – she had sketched a perfect likeness of Agnes – a woman she had never met – lying in a coffin and on her chest was an object, a brooch. Later that evening the telephone rang. It was Agnes's daughter. She explained that she had been to the church and rung the doorbell but no-one had replied. The purpose of her visit was to tell us that her mother had died. I said, 'I know, she came through to tell us.'

Needless to say, Agnes's daughter was astonished but doubly so when we described the object Dronma had drawn in the picture of her in the coffin: the brooch was the exact one that she had bought for her mother and one she had already decided would be a treasured keepsake. By showing it to us, Agnes had proved that it was indeed her who had come through.

*****

BUT back to fear. Being gay presented me with huge fears. For one thing, it meant leaving a life of marital safety. But I had to do that or I would have been trapped by my fear. To be happy you must first be fearless. What's the worst thing that could happen? People may dislike you, they may even hate you but that's none of your business, it won't kill you – such deep resentments might kill them, though.

Being fearless is not the same as being brave, it is simply lacking fear. Being afraid cannot change the outcome of any given situation. If you are on a plane and you are afraid that it might crash, accept the fact that there is nothing you can do to avert it: you are not the pilot. Just sit back and enjoy the ride. And that's true of life.

Look in the mirror every morning and remind yourself, 'I have nothing to fear but fear itself. It cannot even exist unless I let it. Today I will accept the things I cannot change.'

Acceptance is a big part of my life's philosophy today. An old man once said to me, 'Son, do you know what I do if I look through the curtains first thing in the morning and it's pouring with rain out there? ... I let it.'

Wow.

9

Courage

DOING what I do, I see some amazing examples of courage. One that personifies this is that of a young gay man whom I saw in Gibraltar. He had AIDS and he wanted to know about dying. He was quite ill, he had started to develop sores and he had welts on his tongue. He told me his partner, Diego, was in the Spirit world, having died of the illness. Diego came through and gave him a beautiful message. Now the reason I say he had great courage is the extremely practical way he looked on his impending death. He was not afraid, he simply wanted to know if Diego would be there when he crossed to the Other Side.

His family and friends wanted nothing to do with him because this was when the AIDS scare was at its height and people were terrified of it and treated sufferers like lepers. He said to me, 'I don't care about dying. I am alive today and sure as hell I am going to live and go beyond this AIDS thing. I want to teach people about it because it's not what they think.' He really wanted to make people understand that it was not something dirty but an illness, just as cancer is an illness. He had it and he had nursed his partner until he died of it

He was amazing and I was lifted by his spirit. I said to him, 'Good for you. You are not actually dying of AIDS, you are living with it and that is very courageous.'

I told him Diego was saying it would be some time yet but they would be reunited. I also told him that Diego was saying something about some shoes he had left behind, to which the young man said, 'I'm wearing them, tell him they're very comfortable!' After he had gone I thought, *If ever I am hit with something like that, I hope I can be as brave*, and I often wonder if he was able to achieve his ambition to convince others with the message he wanted to deliver from *this* side.

*****

FOR obvious reasons, I suppose, death seems to be on everybody's mind when they come to see me. During the question-and-answer session of a demonstration I gave a few months ago in Glasgow, a man in the audience asked me, 'What happens when we die?' That was a pretty broad question because, as I explained to him, everybody's death is as different as everybody's life. But those I have spoken to who have had near-death experiences tell me that they felt either as though they were being lifted out of their body or that they had the sensation of passing very quickly through a tunnel. Most say they felt illuminated at some point.

I have heard descriptions of such people being surrounded by family and friends who had previously died. Thanks to the generosity of another medium, Leslie Flint, who was able to bring through voices of the dead, I was able to listen to the tapes of a boy telling his mother what it was like to die. He was killed in a car accident and described it thus: 'All of a sudden I felt as though I had fainted and then I felt myself move up and away from my body but I could barely recognize it as my body. I looked down on the scene of the accident and thought, *Look at all those people down there, what's happening to them?* The next thing I knew I was surrounded and bathed in a warming light. It took a while to adjust [to the sense of touch] because I didn't have a body any more but I did and do know that I am alive. I feel connected.'

But that, as I explained to my inquisitor, was his experience. Others I have heard of have been very different but I have yet to hear of one that was unpleasant. It's like asking what heaven – if that's how you regard the Other Side – is like. Spirits' descriptions differ as much as ours would if, say, someone who lived in the South American jungle were to describe his or her version of what life on earth is like and then you compared that to someone who was born and bred in New York City.

*****

I ENJOY the question-and-answer sessions because they test me and are unfailingly interesting to me. So here's some more from the Glasgow Q&A:

A man said he was getting a very clear message about when his desperately ill father was going to die, to enter the Spirit world, and asked what he should do with this information. I told him that that does happen to people whose antennae is such that they are good recipients of information from beyond the norm. It might well be so that he can prepare for the loss. I rarely get times and dates of this nature but when I do I don't pass them on and I urged this man not to tell his father. We are all going to die but to be given a date is not a good thing.

A woman asked me when I first realized I had psychic powers and if it was when I was cutting someone's hair? I explained that it was when I was quite young, long before I became a hairdresser but I did realize the full impact of it when women started bringing their husbands to the salon with orders to question me on psychic matters.

Another woman said her eldest son was a policeman who regarded all things psychic as rubbish but was unable to explain his twice-experienced sensation of being held down in his bed by a force which was not evident. This, I told her, was a common phenomenon which was often associated with out-of-body experiences (you will have read about mine in Chapter 3), something that happens when the mind detaches from the body.

The sister of a woman who finds it very difficult to move on after suffering a loss wanted to know if the Spirits would still come to her, because she was nervous and if they did would it make her more nervous? Spirits, I explained, have no wish to frighten any of us. And because of that they would try and find a more subtle way of communicating if they wanted to get a message through. People often frighten themselves and blame the Spirits, especially if, say, something moves in a room. That's usually a case of someone projecting his or her own fears, which have nothing to do with the departed.

I was able to tell a lady who wanted to know why only some Spirits come through to people like myself while many on this side are waiting for others: first, not every Spirit can work through every medium. I can't get a message for everyone who comes to me because not all Spirits think I am the appropriate person for them to communicate through.

Second, the Spirits are usually respectful of each other. One who is waiting to come through will see the greater need of another who is able to pass on information about, say, a sister who has gone missing. It should also be remembered – and this is important – that a message delivered to an individual might well give something to others who are present and that's one of the reasons we give demonstrations. Many who have not had a direct message will nevertheless take something from a public meeting. It's the ripple effect of what we do.

A particularly interesting question came from a woman who wanted to know how we could best make ourselves open to Spirits anxious to come through. I get asked this a lot and first I explain that we do not and should not attempt to call up the Spirits. The best way to attract a Spirit is to think of people as being alive, not dead. During my last American tour a woman said to me, 'I've been crying over my mother's death for nine years now and she still hasn't come through to me. Why not?' I asked her, 'When did you last think of your mother's *life*? Your mother did more in her life than just die. When you start concentrating on her life rather than her death then you will allow her to be alive. You are killing her again and again by saying she's dead.' Once you've done that you are ready to communicate positively. Ask them to, say, touch your head or give you something that you will recognize their presence by and wait until you get that. But never give them the 'Prove it' ultimatum. That kills off communication altogether. They are there and we must not doubt it if we want to have some contact with them.

'Can Spirits becomes nuisances?' asked another. 'No,' I said, 'people can become nuisances,' but I also had to admit that on occasions I have told the Spirits to go away when, for example, I wanted to go back to sleep and they were crowding my head. This type of thing happened to me before I had developed the ability to switch off. If I didn't tell them to leave they would plague me the whole night. It's not their fault; after all, in the early days I was encroaching on their world.

On a more serious note, schizophrenics have been known to blame the symptoms of their terrible illness on Spirits. I had a guy who asked me to be an expert witness at his trial after he had attacked his GP when the GP had said that he needed to be hospitalized. He was seriously schizophrenic and the doctor thought he should be sectioned under the Mental Health Act. It was somebody in his family who phoned me and said, 'We would like you to come to Edinburgh. There's a trial and we would like to call you as an expert witness because we are sure that our brother has been plagued by Spirits. You must have heard of cases like this where the Spirits are to blame.' When the caller told me what her brother had done I said, 'No way. The Spirits simply don't do things like that. Your brother clearly needs medical help.' And the woman got abusive to me on the phone.

I will not repeat here the language of abuse I got. The sister refused to accept that Spirits never tell anyone to attack anyone. That is simply bad behaviour. All too often I hear of people hearing voices and blaming their subsequent actions on those from the Other Side. It may well be that schizophrenia can cause people to behave in certain anti-social ways, but that's not the Spirits.

Why, someone asked me, are animals on 'different vibrations' and does this make it hard for them to communicate with us? The second part of the question is pointless because the answer to the first is, 'They are not.' I don't know where some people get the idea that God has decided to put animals in a separate realm. Whilst they obviously cannot talk, I get the sense of animals on the Other Side all the time and can often get the name of a pet when it is in the company of a loved one, even a projection of its nature. There are some animals which are more openly conscious and better developed in the Spirit world than some people. The late husband of a woman I saw in London not so long ago came through and told me that he had been killed in a plane crash (which his widow confirmed). I told her he was surrounded by dogs; not Collies or Labradors but wild African dogs. 'That's right,' she said. 'My husband kept them on a game reserve he owned in South Africa.' How significant that those dogs should have made their presence felt just as I conveyed the Spirit's message to his widow.

Yet another animal lover's message went to a lady whose dog, a West Highland terrier, I was being told, had been kicked to death by a horse. 'My God, that's exactly what happened,' said the woman. 'Well,' I said, 'not to worry, your aunt says she has the dog with her and they are both fine.'

I've delivered many, many messages where animals have come through. Not just dogs but rabbits and even parrots.

A woman asked if children come through to me. The answer was, 'Yes, lots of children come through, especially if they are good communicators. As with adults it depends a lot on their powers of communication. Obviously babies cannot do that but from them I can get feelings and emotions just as you would if they were here in this life.'

*****

THE questions I got asked on my first trip to America came as quite a surprise – perhaps shock would be a better word. I went to Boston in 2001 and began the tour with some private sittings – they are pretty much the same the world over, with people anxious to communicate with loved ones they have lost. The following day I worked in a beautiful Spiritualist church in one of the city's prettiest suburbs. The atmosphere was fabulous, so all was well. It wasn't until a couple of days later that I gave a demonstration in a big hall run by an organisation called the Spiritualist Association that I got my eye-opener.

The place felt showbizy and I certainly wasn't in a showbusiness mood. Very early on I got the impression that what I do is not what they had turned up for; they wanted what are known as readings – 'Can you tell me if the sale of my house is going to go through?' 'Is my son going to pass his exams?'

I was growing increasingly concerned when something amazing happened – something which has changed my outlook on America and, I believe, America's view of me. The reaction of one woman to my disclosure that her mother was coming through was, 'Yeah, but what about my brother – is he going to keep his job?' I stopped for a few moments and suddenly you could hear a pin drop as I said to the Spirits, 'Come on, give me a message here. I need help.' Almost immediately my prayer was answered. I got a message for a man in the audience whom I could see. He was a well-dressed, well-educated man who had gone along with his wife and, it turned out, was very sceptical about the whole thing. 'I have a message for you, sir,' I began. 'It is from your father. He is telling me that he is Greek, he was in fact a fisherman who was born and lived his life in Corfu. He is telling me that you are a dentist and he is very proud of the status you have achieved in this country.' And on and on the information flowed. From that point on the audience listened in silence except, of course, when I sought responses from anyone I was delivering to.

Later the dentist came up to thank me and actually told me he had been 'blown away' by the experience. 'I've seen a lot of you guys,' he said, 'but you're different. You don't know me and you couldn't possibly have known about my father being a Corfu fisherman. Thank you so much.' But his gratitude to me was no greater than mine to him. It gave me the confidence to do in America what I do here – the one thing I believe I was born to do – to put people in touch with those they have lost to the Other Side and not get pulled in the direction audiences might otherwise have had me go.

In Britain mediums are taught that we are there to give people evidence, not to answer questions and give the kind of information fortune tellers offer.

Even now when I am in the United States people call out questions when I am giving messages but I have the confidence to get on with my work and very quickly they understand and respect that. I set out my stall and make it clear that that's what's on offer. Often they will approach me when the demonstration is over and say, 'Well, that's amazing. You really do talk to the dead.' It may not be what they're used to but it's what they can expect from me.

*****

I DON'T believe in testing people's courage by giving them dire news. A woman once asked me if she was going to die. I could see her dead in my head and I knew it would only be a matter of days but I wasn't about to tell her even when she persisted with the question, adding, 'Tell me because I've got things to do.' 'Look,' I said, 'we're all going to die. You can either spend whatever time you have left living and doing the things you want to do and saying the things you need to say to people, or you can sit and wonder when you're going to die. So you're either active in living what time you have left on earth, or not. It's up to you.'

Still she persisted: 'Will it only be days?' and I said, 'I have no idea, nobody gives me great insight into the time of death.' I had a feeling her death was imminent but what would have been the point in telling her that? It would have wasted the precious little time she had left. That is the only instance where I won't tell exactly what I'm feeling as I see it.

Once, though, I did break every rule in the book to give a woman news I personally wasn't sure of. She was, and still is, I'm happy to say, a friend, and she had a number of cancerous tumours. She came to Jim and me for healing and after a few sessions her doctor said to her, 'I don't know what it is you are doing but you're getting better; you're really coming along and I have to say we didn't expect this.'

So she told him she was having Spiritual healing and he said, 'Good, that's a good thing. It obviously helps.' So she was in remission and felt great for five years or so but when she went back for some reconstructive surgery, they noticed from the X-ray that she had a massive tumour behind the ear, so close to the brain that it was inoperable and she was told that she would be dead within three weeks.

Anyway, she called me and told me that she'd accepted the awful news but she was very worried about the little dog that she had recently taken from an animal rescue centre and which she loved so much. 'What am I going to do?' she said. 'I don't care what it costs but that dog is so attached to me and I am so worried about what will happen to it. Would you come and try some more healing for me?'

She pointed out that she was not expecting me to save her life, she just wanted to feel comfortable about what would happened to her dog when she passed on. She came round, we chatted for a while and I had just started the healing when Albert Best – who had passed on by this time – appeared. 'She's not dying, Gordon,' he said. I looked at the woman and said in my thoughts, *I can't tell her that, Albert*, but he just repeated, 'She's not dying.' So in my head I'm having this argument with Albert. I was saying that I could never give anybody false hope.

Then, standing beside Albert I saw this elderly oriental man whom I knew to be his guide and healer, and this man was showing me an X-ray and repeating what Albert had said: 'She's not dying.'

Horrible though it is, I would prefer to tell someone they should prepare for death rather than give them false hope, so my stomach was in knots as I turned to the woman and said: 'I'm going to tell you something that I am getting from the Spirit world: within ten days you are going to be told that you are not dying.' She laughed out loud and said, 'Gordon, now I know you're crazy; you've just been transferred to the circle where I keep the dafter side of my friends. My boss said you were a crank and that I should stay away from you!'

'I promise you I wouldn't say this if I didn't mean it,' I said. I felt the colour drain from my face and she looked at me and said, 'My God, you really mean it, don't you?' I assured her that I was absolutely serious, that I would bet my own life on it. Shortly after she left I confided what had happened to an old friend – a mutual one as it happens – who said: 'Christ, Gordon, I trust most things you do but that was disgusting.' I felt awful.

Ten days later, however, she called me in hysterics to say, 'Gordon. You were right! They were looking at someone else's X-ray when they made that diagnosis. I'm still in remission!' Then the mutual friend phoned to say he believed he owed me an apology. 'Too right,' I said. 'I stuck my neck out there and you all but destroyed my confidence, my faith.'

Another who had had no faith was the woman's boss. But he phoned in tears when he heard the whole story. It had, he admitted, brought him down off his high horse.

The woman is alive and well today. Thank you, Albert.

*****

TO be honest, I don't think my mother and father have ever come to terms with what it is I do. They can't quite get their heads around it. There are certain bits they like – my father was at the doctor's recently and somebody asked him to get me to sign something and he did like that. They also like it when I'm on TV or doing a book signing. Both my parents are proud working-class people who live in the real world and at times think my life to be 'out there somewhere'.

When people ask her what it is I do, Mum tells them I'm a holy person, she says I help people. She has been to my demonstrations and her comments afterwards have ranged from, 'It's nice what you do, son,' to, 'Did that really happen?' When she was young she wanted to be a dancer or a singer so I have a sneaking suspicion that she'd like to be up there on stage with me.

My father's thinking changed radically last spring when he had an experience that defied his normally rational way of seeing things. Dad suffers from a really serious chest problem – he has asbestosis. A recent attack was so serious that he was rushed to hospital. Initially he was delirious but then, he said, everything went calm and, 'It was like a light coming on.' Then, this tough, practical man whom as children we had to watch in silence as he ate his tea after a hard day's work, says he saw before him his sister Alice who had died years earlier. 'She came up to me and said, "I know you," and he said, "Yes, Alice, I'm your brother." She just smiled and everything was beautiful,' he said. 'I can see her there as plainly as I can now see you, son.' The next thing he knew he came to and found himself lying on the floor with the nurses struggling to pick him up. He had stepped forward to touch his sister, but, crippled with arthritis, he'd just keeled over.

Afterwards he had a clutch of questions for me, questions he would never have asked me before this experience: 'What happened to me?' 'Was that real?' 'Is that what I can expect when this life ends?' Now this is a very down-to-earth man who, if someone got religious in the house, would say, 'There's that woman who preaches to us and she's drunk tonight and she'll be going to the chapel tomorrow to beg forgiveness. You don't need to go to church to be good.' Yet here he was, the stable centre of our family, the man who taught me to read, to tell the time and to tie my shoelaces, asking me to explain a very real Spiritual experience he had had.

He asked me if he had been close to death and when I said, 'Yes,' my mother said, 'That's a terrible thing to say to your father, don't talk like that.' 'But, Mum,' I protested, 'he *was* close to death,' and my father cut in: 'Yes, I believe it and if that's what it will be like when I die, that's great. I only wish it would hurry up because I can't get my breath and now I can see I have nothing to fear about what lies ahead.' My father has always been the person in my life who taught me never to fear life or death. He is a good man and someone I consider very wise. He has never feared death and now I know he has no fear of what lies beyond that veil.

I had long told my father that I don't just believe there is life after death, I *know* there is; and suddenly he knew it too.

*****

I AM often asked if either of my sons has inherited the Gift and it does not sadden me in the least to say no. They are both bright boys and, I believe, are destined to have far more normal lives than the one I am having. Paul recently took a second degree at Glasgow University and Steven is still working out just what he would like to do – a happy place to be.

When they lived at home their friends used to come and visit and I am happy to report that I was considered 'cool'. Being a medium was different so it was a cool thing to do. One teenage boy came to me once and said, 'If I had a problem, could you tell what it was and give me the answer without me telling you what the question was?' I said, 'It's all right, she's not pregnant. But be careful in future.' He was clearly impressed but that had nothing to do with my abilities as a medium, just a fatherly figure who was once a teenager himself.

*****

IT'S not often that delivering messages from the Other Side is a hazardous business, but it can happen. The whole family came along with a very emotional lady when I gave her a sitting during my Italian sojourn – families often do in Italy. What's more, it was a family that reminded me of growing up on the wild side of Glasgow.

'You have a daughter in the Spirit world,' I told her. 'She died of kidney cancer. Her name was Michela.' '*Sì, sì, sì,*' she said, getting to the edge of her seat. I did what I could to avoid eye contact because I could see this was going to be a tough sitting for her and maybe for me too.

As I went into further detail, saying the daughter had died in her twenties, she began to scream, 'Michela! Michela is here!' And with that she left the edge of the seat and, screaming and pulling her hair with one hand, grabbed me round the neck with the other, practically throttling me until the family managed to pull her off.

I explained to the family via the translator that she would need to control such emotional outburst if I was going to be able to deliver the message I was getting for her. It was a beautiful message. Michela knew that her mother prayed to the Virgin for her every day and when I mentioned Padre Pio she screamed again, 'Padre Pio is with her?' When I told her he was she sobbed uncontrollably.

It was a beautiful message but I needed a strong drink after I had delivered it; some people can get so emotionally involved.

I got quite the opposite kind of reaction in a small town between Bologna and Assisi when a woman, dressed in an apron and headscarf and looking as though she had just stepped away from her chores, came by for a sitting. She gave me a very tough look that said, 'Prove it,' rather than, 'Help me.' *Oh no*, I thought once again, *what am I getting into here?* Anyway, I started, pausing only for the translator to interpret every few sentences: 'You have lost a son. He died in a mysterious way, it was not a normal death. The boy was shot at one stage, but lived only to be stabbed and beaten on another occasion. Eventually he died through some kind of poisoning, I think he is saying lethal injection.'

It was only when I said, 'His name was Massimo,' that she began to show any kind of reaction.

'I see a woman rising from his bed, producing a syringe from her handbag and stabbing him with it. Bang! It was instant death. The woman fled.' Now the sitter relaxed, muttering long sentences beneath her breath and crossing herself.

'Your son is here,' I said. 'He says you told him this woman would be bad for him and he told you to [I have deleted the expletive].' The woman nodded solemnly as the translator conveyed this to her and then she began to talk at length and it was the translator's turn to turn Italian into English.

'She says you are right, Mr Gordon. Her son got mixed up in some petty crime in the town but he did not run with the gang. Time and time again they tried to punish him for that. He survived a shooting and a stabbing and then came this girl, this beautiful blonde who was obviously not from these parts. The words [the expletives] you used were the last he uttered to his mother before he left her house for the last time and she repeated them back to him. She believes it was the woman who killed him on behalf of his enemies. The woman disappeared. No-one can trace her.'

I interrupted him. I was getting more of the message from the Other Side: 'You visit his grave every day and he says, yes, the rose you found there one morning had been placed by the woman. She had been there the previous night.'

When this was translated the mother swore. And then she got up, nodded her head at me and left.

It has to be said that I have had some of my most dramatic experiences in Italy. One man who came to see me in northern Italy was by no stretch of the imagination the normal sort to visit a medium. He was sharply dressed and extremely businesslike and I would normally have asked him if he'd lost anyone, in other words if he had any business being there at all. But the Spirit of an elderly woman appeared almost immediately, so I realized he had.

It was the last sitting of the day on what had been a very busy week and working constantly through interpreters clearly adds to the strain. 'She tells me her name is Franca, she is your aunt and that you have come a long way for me to put you in touch with her,' I said (in fact he had travelled all the way up from Sicily for this sitting). She says you have control over your father's business and your father is with her, saying you are doing well [I was later told by the translator that the 'family business' was organized crime]. She says she died in Switzerland of natural causes although she doesn't think you believe that.'

He nodded in agreement at all the information I gave him but I sensed that he was growing impatient – I was not asking the questions he had come for answers to.

Finally his impatience got the better of him: 'Never mind that, ask her for the numbers, what are the numbers?' I was confused but the reply from the Other Side was the name and rough location of a bank in Geneva. 'I know that,' said the man. 'I want the numbers, the numbers of the accounts.'

But just as suddenly as it had come through, the Spirit was gone. The man had travelled all this way to try and locate the details of Swiss bank accounts in which the aunt had placed much of the family business's cash – and I suspected by now that the family business was dubious, to say the least.

After his aunt had left, his father came through and my sitter told me to ask him if there was now no longer any need to deal with the people who were close to his aunt when she met her death. Imagine the horror: I was dealing here with people who had little respect for life and were probably heavily involved in crime.

Despite my failure to get him what he wanted, he offered me a job in Sicily. I explained as tactfully as I could that I already had my own hairdressing business in Scotland but would call on him the very next time I was in Sicily.

*****

THE ability to pick up bad vibes and foretell when there's trouble ahead has saved my bacon so many times, and that's one thing a pseudo medium could never count on. Jim and I once went to a party at the home of a friend of ours called Alan. Alan throws great parties and this was a massive one and looked like being lots of fun, but I had not been there long before I sensed that there was something wrong. Kim, who worked with me at the hairdressers and who is also a healer, felt the same, so the three of us decided to go. As we left, three guys arrived and for no reason that I could comprehend, my stomach lurched. We learned later that they had stabbed someone. If he ever did before, Jim has never doubted my instinct since.

*****

NOT everybody to whom I pass a message has asked for it. One of my favourite stories – because it was such a happy one – is set in the salon of my barber's shop. I was going about my trade – giving a chap a shave on this occasion – when a very pretty, very chic young woman appeared in the mirror. I knew the customer would not be able to see what I could, although it was right there in front of his face, so I just looked and listened.

She had short blonde hair tucked behind her ears, wore a very nice black cocktail dress, her name was Judy and she was very interested in my customer. I took the bull by the horns and said, 'This might sound silly, but I am a medium and I believe you have just lost a lady called Judy.' It was just as well I had removed the razor from his face because he shot bolt upright, paused for a moment and then burst into tears. Finally he spoke: 'How did you know that?' and in the way that I had learned to ask the Spirits for information at times like this, I thought, *Show me something, Judy, something that will make him believe it is you.* 'Thanks,' she said in my mind, 'for the lollipops,' and with that she was gone.

When I verbalized the thought, he was dumbfounded. He told me the story. Judy had died suddenly, leaving him to bring up their young son. Earlier that week he had taken the boy on their regular trip to the cemetery, only this time the lad had asked if, instead of flowers, he could take Mummy some lollipops.

I was as amazed as my customer (who, by the way, had walked into the shop just as I was preparing to pack up and leave, so it was almost a fluke that I was able to serve him).

When you're a psychic barber, as I once was called, you just never know who is going to come by – on either side.

10

Don't Blame The Spirits

THERE is, I never tire of telling people, no such thing as a haunted house, only haunted people. On the recent UK tour, I remember a lady in the audience at Newcastle asking me if people in the Spirit world can hurt us by making us feel frightened or uncomfortable. I answered by telling her that I had never come up against anything in the Spirit world which I would consider evil or frightening. A white shirt hung over a door in a dark room remains a white shirt. When a radiator makes a noise, it's not a ghost, it's a radiator with air in the pipes; when a door rattles, it's a loose handle. Often it's our mind that projects images of fear and attaches them to noises and objects when we are afraid, not the Spirit world. When we are afraid our Spirit loved ones would never add to that by appearing

Having said all that, I will go on to point out that the Spirits are capable of acts which might appear frightening to those who do not understand their way of communicating. These are usually warnings or at least messages for us to be prepared.

Not too long ago Jim and I were walking with our late dog Charlie in some woods we were familiar with in a place called Hillington when we came across Craigton Cemetery.

Charlie ran in and scampered off to an ancient part of the burial ground where the graves were all at least a century old. Suddenly we heard him whining at the top of his voice. He always came back when we called him but on this occasion he wouldn't, so we were obliged to go and find him. He was standing in front of a headstone which bore the inscription, 'Gordon Smith, author,' and below that 'Steven Andrew Smith, able seaman, died at sea 1917.'

My youngest son, whose first two names are Steven Andrew, had recently joined the Royal Navy and he was hating it. He had phoned home asking if we could find a lawyer who would get him out of the service. The Navy resisted because he is very bright and his superior wanted to get him on an officers' course. Eventually, however, he was allowed to leave and shortly afterwards America invaded Iraq – a war in which he might well have become involved.

A couple of months later, Jim and I again found ourselves in the Hillington area and decided to pay a return visit to Craigton Cemetery and that grave. The late author's name was still on the headstone but instead of Steven Andrew Smith beneath his name it read Daphne Smith, daughter of Gordon Smith. The carving was very old and could not possibly have been tampered with.

Make of that what you will.

*****

THESE days the Spirits disturb my sleep less and less. Before, when I was in a half-sleep, they would frequently interrupt it, but when I learned to take control of my mind and say, 'Enough!' they seemed to get my message.

I still, however, have vivid memories of times when they have rattled my cage in more senses than one. About four years ago I had just finished a particularly busy schedule and went to bed on this particular night feeling absolutely exhausted. To try and ensure I got the long sleep I so desperately needed I got the room as dark as I possibly could. My head was numb. When you do a lot of mediumship you reach a stage where you just can't think any more and that's the state I was in this night. My forehead felt as if it was unplugged; there was nothing, no spark.

Now often when I get like that I begin to see and hear things because the control of my mind is relaxed and I am vulnerable to Spirits I could otherwise dispatch by saying, 'Enough.' I remember on this occasion, however, feeling footsteps in the room. *Oh no*, I thought, *who is this?* Then I felt someone kneel first at the side of the bed and then lean over my chest – quite a heavy weight it was too. I decided to keep my eyes closed, having considered that if I opened them I would see someone and I preferred to sense them as then there is no issue of focus.

Then I spoke. I said out loud, 'What do you want?' I sensed that it was a young man leaning on my chest; I could feel him breathing on me, he was that close. Then, in my mind's eye, I saw a scene in what was obviously a Spiritualist church. I was on the rostrum and at the very back were a young man and a woman. Suddenly a shadowy figure moved towards them and put his hand on the young man's shoulder. Just as suddenly the scene switched to an open road and a motorcyclist slewing across it. There had been an accident, he had been killed. And then I fell into the deepest of deep sleeps.

So intense was my sleep that when I woke the following morning it was like my mind had been cleansed and at that point I had no memory of the previous night's happenings. Then the telephone rang and a voice said, 'Where were you last night? You were due here at the church in Kilmarnock.' 'No,' I said, 'I've got it in my diary for tonight, I'm coming tonight.' I had made a mistake with my diary entries but the caller said, 'No problem, we got another medium to stand in for you last night so we'll see you tonight.'

I got to Kilmarnock and had no sooner sat on the rostrum when I saw at the back of the church the young couple who had appeared in the previous night's experience. It all came back to me in a flash. It was so vivid, so real, so unlike a dream. When the introduction, prayers and hymn singing had finished I could contain myself no longer: 'Excuse me, the boy at the back, you've lost a brother in a motorcycle accident,' and with that the force that had leaned on my bed, on my chest the previous night, came through and I was able to describe how he had died, and to provide evidence that it was indeed this young man's brother. There was no reason for him coming to me but he was desperate to get through to his brother on this side and he had been able to get through to me because my defences were down and I had no control, no way of stopping him.

It's amazing when I look at the synchronicity of these things. He had come to me on that particular night because I should have been in the church and able to deliver his message there and then. It made me wonder if that happened to me a lot. Do people come and converse with me when I am in a sleep state so that I am prepared to deliver their messages later? It sounds bizarre but, I concluded, it could well be the case. That's what I was meant to learn that night: that when I am asleep they are preparing me for what lies ahead. I know it has happened on other occasions when I have been exhausted but perhaps it happens a lot when I am out for the count: that Spirits arrive in my thoughts and say, 'Tomorrow my father/son/daughter or whoever will be there. Be prepared.'

*****

I AM not an evangelist seeking a following and I am not a religion. A lot of seekers of Spiritualism also follow a religion quite devotedly. It has been said in the past that religion is for people who don't want to go to hell and Spiritualism is for people who've been there. I would put it even more simply: Spiritualism is about proving that there is an afterlife, and providing the evidence is what I do as a medium.

I was not brought up in any particular religion. As I've said, although my father's family were Protestants and my mother's Catholic, neither of them practised any faith but they certainly had a go at each other when arguments about religious dogma came up. We weren't atheists and as a boy I used to sneak into the chapel a lot because I was curious; only to be recognized by the priest and removed.

The funny thing is, prayer came naturally to me – my form of prayer, that is. I would wish for people to get better and that to me is a better form of prayer than asking for something for yourself. And seemingly as a result I knew when my prayers were going to be answered and I could tell people when things were going to get better. 'How do you know?' they would say. 'Because I know,' I would reply, unable to explain the answers I received in this inner world I had occupied since childhood.

So to me prayer was a natural thing; I never had to be taught how to do it. I talk to God and, no, I don't get on my knees to do it because to me that suggests you are beneath God and I don't think that is what it's all about. The God of my understanding is not one who obliges you to humble yourself before Him. That school of thought just doesn't make sense to me and again a lot of people in their own prayer life tend to beg for things. Something I learned earlier was that you don't do that, you ask for something and if it happens, it happens – your prayer's been answered. I once heard Sylvia Browne, the American medium I sometimes work with, being asked by a woman who had been getting on her knees every night to beg God for something: 'Why won't He answer my prayers?' To which Sylvia replied: 'He has. He's said "No."'

*****

THERE is nothing wrong with religion, any religion, except that to me it is a field which has perimeters and you are kept in that field by your belief, and at some point people will see that there is a huge expanse beyond their field of belief and that they are held within that field by its doctrine. The sad thing about religion is that there is nothing wrong with Christianity, for example, except the Christians. I would say the same for Spritualists. Spiritualism is in itself a lovely free doctrine which tells you that you will always grow, given a chance and if you're pointed in the right direction; it's just you who stops yourself going any further. So what I tell people is, don't limit your mind by putting up the barriers that, say, your parents used to fence themselves in. Stories of what might or might not have happened in long-gone times govern too many people too much of the time. Belief has no perimeters.

I used to get a lot of religious people coming up to me after demonstrations, asking about evil Spirits and saying, 'What does Jesus think of this?' 'I don't know,' I'd answer. They'd persist: 'Does Jesus come into this at all?' and to them I would say, 'Have you listened to anything I've said?' because they clearly hadn't. What I talk about goes beyond religious doctrine. It does not, however, exclude it.

*****

HAVING said that I am not a religious practitioner, I would point out that from time to time I do find myself in a similar position to a priest hearing confession.

At a book signing not long ago, a woman in the line started to ask me a very disguised question and I sensed that she was seriously troubled by something she did not wish to relate in such a public gathering; so I suggested we had a private chat later.

The story she told me illustrated just why she had looked so worried. Many years earlier a child had been murdered and the family suspected that this woman's father was the killer. He had always denied it but on his deathbed he had confessed to her that it was indeed him. She had no idea what to do with this horrible dark secret.

Now the father was dead. He could not be tried for the crime and the case could never be proven. But he had committed another terrible sin – he had passed the burden of his guilt on to his daughter. My message to her that night was to carry the burden no longer. She could not be responsible for his actions and she needed to know that she had no part in or responsibility for the matter. A priest might have said she went away absolved!

*****

TO the atheist who wants to believe that there is life after death but cannot bring himself to believe in a God of any description, I suggest that he accepts there must be something, someone more powerful than himself. I would ask him if he could make a blade of grass or knew anyone else who could. If he is honest, the answer would have to be 'No' on both counts. But he does not need to look far to see millions of such blades growing in any field or lawn, surely made by a power greater than him if he admits he cannot do it. That's a start. To the man who says he has no faith in anything, I ask him what he expects to happen when he presses a light switch. He surely has faith that the action will turn the light on. That's a good start too.

*****

OF course, Spiritualism sometimes enrages practitioners of other religions, although no more so than Catholics and Muslims and so on do. It's not often that I have to do battle with a priest but it happened in Gibraltar when I went back there to do a demonstration at a large theatre to help raise funds for a hospice. No sooner had I arrived than I was listening to a radio news report declaring, 'The devil has arrived in Gibraltar.' Who, I wondered, can that be? Didn't have to wonder long – it was me they were talking about.

A Catholic priest regarded me as demonic and had told the local papers that I was the Antichrist. The local media soon located me and asked me if I would take part in a television debate with the priest that evening. Of course I would. The man didn't have a leg to stand on. He began with a huge error: 'You, Mr Smith, are a scientologist ...' 'Don't be daft,' I said, perhaps a little irreverently. 'I am nothing of the kind and you would know that had you done any research into who I am and what I do. Look, here's the deal, I'm a medium and in the UK Spiritualism is a bona fide religion and I am a practitioner of that religion. I am not here to tell people anything against God, I am not an Antichrist and I am not a devil. I am here to talk about life after death. It's Satanism, not Spiritualism, that declares there is no afterlife, so can you answer that?'

He responded with a double negative: 'I didn't know you weren't a scientologist.'

'Well, you know now,' I said. 'Many of your parishioners came to see me on my last visit here and many of them benefited from what I was able to say. And furthermore, what we are doing tonight is not to benefit me but a hospice. What are you doing to raise funds for it?'

'But,' he blustered, 'you're calling up Spirits, the devil himself.'

'I'm doing nothing of the sort,' I retorted. 'I'm helping your parishioners here who are grieving. I'm not saying you can't help them but they choose to come to me. I don't ask them to, I'm here and if they want to come they are welcome. But what are you doing, why can't you help?' Then he declared: 'It says in the Bible you can't call up Spirits.' I told him I didn't care what it said and where; I knew I was doing a good thing. And then I invited him to the event he was trying to sabotage: 'Why don't you come along and learn something tonight?'

He didn't show up, of course, but when he spoke to the papers later on he'd changed his tune. He said he understood that I was not there to do any harm after all but had in fact come to help a good cause. In actual fact I had given him a private message afterwards, off-air, which made him feel like a bit of a hypocrite. Not only did I have no further bother with him, but because of the furore he had caused, ticket sales swelled from 200 to 1,000 and the place was packed for the demonstration.

Most of the people who came were those who had lost children and they were looking for answers that they couldn't find in the Church. And that wasn't to say that what I was doing was better than his Church; they had been brought up in a faith and I was trying to point them back to their faith.

*****

I HAD a similar problem more recently with a priest in Britain, who said that while he believed that mediums could contact the dead, they did not know exactly who was feeding them with the information they provided. It could, he said, be an evil source drawing the bereaved towards evil. 'Why,' I argued, 'would they want to help people so much in the first place if they were evil?'

Some healers do in fact draw negative energies towards themselves in order to dissipate it. They extract demons in the form of doubt, fear, anger, greed, hatred and suchlike from people who have been made ill by such things. Somebody who is bitter is ill, and if you are afraid of the demons in them, then you will be affected by that person's negativity.

Healers who are not sufficiently qualified will take on the sufferer's pain, and they may show it because they have a need to be seen to be helping. Someone who is more practised can take on the pain and get rid of it very quickly. They don't advertise that they are doing it, you don't even tell the person you are helping that that's what you are doing.

Novices make a big fuss about it in order to get attention: 'Oh dear, I put my hand on your back and took the backache away but now I've got it.' It's human nature for people to want to take credit for what they do. It is not Spiritual nature, though, and that's what we mediums strive for. Don't get me wrong – I know this because I did it myself when I was learning; all the time I wanted people to see how much I was helping.

*****

THERE will always be those who are sceptical about Spiritualism. They don't bother me. I have no time to waste on them, nothing to prove. When I do encounter them I refer them to a BBC documentary made six or seven years ago and called *The Psychic Barber*. Although its title suggests it's all about me; the programme, which has been repeated several times, is a documentary which illustrates the work of Professor

Archie Roy, Professor of Astronomy at Glasgow University and Tricia Robertson, and their research into psychic phenomena.

Although I obviously agreed to go along with it, I had no idea how it would turn out and it wasn't until some time later that I was allowed to see the results of the tests I had been involved in. I had been taken to the university hours before those members of the public who were also taking part. I never saw them and had never met any of them. I was shown into a room which was empty apart from a chair and a table with a microphone on it. No reason to get excited over that, I thought, and promptly fell asleep. Some time later the others taking part were led into another room in another part of the building. I was given a seating plan of a table around which they were sitting and numbers that tallied with the seats they were on. Then I was asked if I saw anything, if I felt anything.

What came out of my mouth was just gibberish as far as I was concerned. I had no idea what it meant. I said that I heard the name John Taylor and he linked with a woman in seat number 15 whose name would also be Taylor and that she had two houses, one of which was called Christmas Cottage, and there was 'The most ridiculously ornate fountain outside the house which he laughs at, and I'm sure it's a private joke between them.'

Later the girls who were making the documentary came to me in a state of some excitement. 'What happened?' I asked. 'You really don't know, do you?' they said. And they were right, I had no idea. In seat 15 had sat John Taylor's widow who lived at Christmas Cottage, the house with the ridiculous fountain.

That was a double blind test – I could not see Mrs Taylor nor was she aware of me and what I was doing. But Professor Roy and Patricia Robertson, vice president of the Scottish Society of Psychical Research, had a triple blind test lined up in which the person I was to identify was not even in the room I was told to concentrate on. In fact, I had no idea what the whole exercise was about.

Patricia merely instructed me to go to the room and said she would come with another witness, hand me a document, and say, 'I want you to make 20 statements about this person.' The person wasn't even there. They would be in another city, at a time in the future. I didn't even know that much at the time. I was just given a questionnaire saying that there were 400 seats in this room and would I be able to tell them who will be in a numbered seat of my choice? It turned out that even they didn't know at that point who would be in which seats, so absolutely no-one was in a position to orchestrate it – to fix it, if you like.

'Patricia,' I began to protest, 'I've got a hangover, we were out drinking last night and …' But she was insistent: 'Just have a go,' she said. I wrote: 'In seat number 170 will be a red-haired woman who has lost her mother. Her name is Mrs Harrison.' I then sealed the piece of paper in an envelope before handing it to Tricia who sealed it in another envelope to post to Professor Roy. He then posted it to the venue so that he could collect it on the day. No risk of tampering there, then. It was very cloak-and-dagger stuff.

Tricia told me later that what I had written turned out to be 98% accurate. It was indeed a red-haired Mrs Harrison who occupied seat 170. They were shocked and I was pleasantly surprised. I hope I have described these tests correctly, but this is how I saw them.

So when sceptics come at me and say, 'There's no evidence to support what you do,' I tell them they are clearly not up on parapsychology or they would know there is such evidence and they should look at it rather than quiz me.

I once confronted (live on Richard and Judy's TV show) a chap called Chris French who is an arch-sceptic of mediums. He was invited on the programme to debunk what I do, and I was pleased about that because he had previously been critical of me without ever having seen what it is I do. He did some tests to try and duplicate what I do and they failed miserably. I had to tell him that as a medium who had taken part in carefully monitored scientific tests, his were nowhere near the standard of the Roy/Robertson tests, and no wonder they failed.

At that point Richard Madeley showed an extract from a documentary to be televised that night in which I gave some precise evidence to a couple I had never encountered before. Richard asked French how he would explain that, and he said he couldn't and then added a strange comment to the effect of me being one of very few he was interested in because he couldn't see 'any rationale' to it. Later he said he would love to conduct further tests with me but I made it clear I wasn't interested, that I had nothing to prove. I feel I have proved it enough; though when Chris and I met again later on the *This Morning* program and again he mentioned doing tests with me, this time I said I might. Chris French is a sceptic that I like; he doesn't just doubt for the sake of it. He really does want to see the genuine article.

But how could he possibly have competed with the carefully monitored scientific experiments conducted by Archie Roy and Patricia Robertson over a seven-year period? How more controlled do you want to be than not even letting me see or be in the same room as the people I am describing or delivering evidence and messages to?

Well, say the sceptics, you must be good at reading body language, at sussing people's thinking from the expressions on their faces. I am actually quite good at doing those things, but the way a man or woman sits and the angle of their mouth doesn't tell me their dead father's name. There have been lots of times when it hasn't worked and I'm sure there's a reason for that which has something to do with my mindset at the time, but you can't manufacture the results I produce most of the time.

I have never asked Professor Roy whether the positive results he got time and time again to his tests turned him into a believer but I did once hear him say, 'If I find out when I die that there is no afterlife, I will be more than disappointed.'

*****

A NURSE on duty in a hospital close to where I once lived called me late at night to say they were treating a dying baby whose mother had asked for a minister, saying she was of the Spiritualist faith. Somehow they got my number and I pointed out that I was not a minister but I was a healer and I would come over and see what I could do. When I arrived the nurse made it clear that they did not expect the baby to last the night.

Needless to say, the mother at the bedside was terribly distraught. The doctors had wanted to operate but Sam, the baby, was in such a bad way that they thought to do so would be counter-productive. I asked the mother if Jim and I might sit with her child and hold its hands. The nurse looked seriously disapproving but did not voice any objections. We did what we could to pass healing to this desperately sick infant and left the mother with our home number, asking her to call at any hour if there was news. When she did call it was to say that Sam's temperature had miraculously returned to normal, the doctors had operated and the prognosis was good.

Jim and I went directly to church to send our thanks. I don't know what the nurse thought of our intervention, but I do know that I was truly grateful our healing prayers seemed to have had an effect.

*****

ONE of the things I had to learn early on was to detach, albeit detach with love. When I started out as a medium I tended to get involved, I would go back to people I had given messages to and ask how they were getting on with their new-found awareness of the Spirit world. Then I came to realize that I was seeking confirmation and this was all about ego. If I didn't ever ask God for anything twice, why should I go back to see if a prayer had been answered unless I was putting my work (or God's) to the test. It certainly wasn't helpful to the people I had tried to help. There comes a point when you must move beyond doubt. What's more, I reasoned, I could not assume that everything I did was right; I am subject to human error as much as the next man. Most importantly I had to learn not to carry other people's grief with me. It's easy to go away feeling desperately sad after you have sat with someone whose daughter has been raped and murdered, but that's not my job. How do I help the next person if I am carrying that one's sorrow?

Another scenario, unless I watch it, is that people can go away feeling good but leaving me as full of misery as they were when they arrived. I have to remind myself that I must not adopt another person's emotions and feelings. Albert Best would say, 'Where's your Cross? You don't need to feel that way; you don't have to take on the world's suffering. Be Gordon. You have given your best and that's the end of it until the next time.' Wise words.

*****

I SAW a couple recently that had never thought of consulting a medium. They had lost their daughter a few months earlier and were deep in grief. By chance the wife happened to be at a meeting which was also attended by Barbara, a lady I had seen the previous week. They had both popped outside for a coffee break when the woman explained her depressed mood: 'I've lost a daughter.' Barbara told her that she had lost a son less than a year ago. The first woman said, 'Well, you look quite bright, considering,' to which the response was, 'Well, I got a lot of help,' and Barbara told her about coming to see me and how I'd got her son back from the Other Side.

'Oh, I would love nothing more than to have that experience,' the woman said, and Barbara promised to ask the lady who had put her in touch with me if I would give her a sitting. Of course I would, was my response.

The woman came with her husband, who was sceptical, to put it mildly. At one stage he said, 'Who are you talking to?

Our daughter's dead.' 'Really? Well, she's talking to you through me,' I explained. The daughter went through a long list of apologies to her parents, including an explanation for her changing moods shortly before she died. I got the impression that she had probably taken her own life but as she didn't volunteer that information, I didn't ask her. My job is to get the parents away from thinking about a corpse and to realize that she is still a living Spirit.

I gave them lots of evidence, including the name of the road they had recently moved to – things I could never have known. The husband was clearly still sceptical and I gave them a tape recording of the sitting so that they could go and listen to it all over again because your memory can play tricks on you at an emotional time like that. Nevertheless he still called Barbara when they got home, to ask, 'Is this guy Gordon for real?' His wife needed no such reassurance. She told Barbara that the communication from her daughter had 'lifted the veil of grief'.

*****

PERSONALLY, I have rarely encountered an angry reaction to any of the thousands of actual messages I have delivered. But I can see where it could happen: a husband, for example, could see his control role diminished when the dread of what has happened to a lost son, daughter, mother or father is removed after his wife has received a message from the loved one – perhaps a message that warns her of danger at home.

A medium friend of mine who had helped just such a woman had to call the police when a man turned up on her doorstep late at night screaming abuse. 'How dare you tell my wife that her late father had told her to face up to me? Who are you to pass on that, you bitch?' was the gist of the message – although I have once again deleted the expletives. He was angry because she had received a message from the Other Side that warned her that unless she took charge of her life it was headed in the wrong direction.

The one occasion on which I did get the 'How dare you?' treatment from a furious sitter, it did not involve any part of the message, but the very fact that I had received it. Here's how it happened. A young man who used to come to one of the development groups I attended at the church asked me if I would see a couple that he knew. He said they were in great distress and he believed that they would benefit greatly from coming to see me, so I agreed and they came along to my house for a private sitting one Saturday morning. Within a very short time I realized exactly who they were. Their daughter had been stabbed to death in the school playground by another girl and the case had been in all the papers.

I said, 'Obviously you must be the parents of this young girl,' and they said they were but I had no idea that their even-younger son had hanged himself as a direct result within a year of the first tragedy.

The sitting from my point of view went extremely well. The girl came through and she was a fantastic communicator and the sitting was all about anger. The parents were still waiting for this other girl to go on trial but their daughter's message to them was, 'Please, this is killing you and no justice that you get is going to take away the hurt unless you start addressing it. Even if she gets a very long sentence, it's not going to make you happy.' I could see what the Spirit meant. The parents up to that point weren't going to be happy unless they saw the other girl dead.

As I finished the sitting the man looked as though a great weight had been taken from his shoulders. He looked really satisfied with his daughter's message but his wife stared me in the face and suddenly burst into an angry tirade: 'How dare you hear my daughter when I can't!' she exploded. She was really angry. She just could not accept that her daughter had been there, that I could hear the girl and she could not.

I felt sick to the stomach when she said that. It was the first time in my life that I had given consideration to the fact that here was a parent who obviously believed I was hearing her daughter but so much so that it angered her. The woman was just filled with anger. Much as I have learned about protecting myself from adopting others' emotions, when they left I felt that a lot of her pain had been transferred to me and my stomach was turning and turning so much that after they had gone I actually threw up. That feeling lay with me a full day and it stayed with me until the following evening's service when I talked about it – not the details of the sitting, of course, but about how the medium can take something like that on and basically about how the effect of the anger that some people carry after a tragic death (or in this case two) can be passed on to others. After all, if I could pick that up after being in their company for just an hour, what must it be like to live their life!

I wasn't even sad; I never get tearful these days. I mean I can walk away and think how awful that was, but I cannot allow myself to get into another person's state of mind. There's a switch off which mediums must have but on this occasion I was certainly badly shaken. It was a great lesson for me, that not only should a medium develop compassion for the people they are trying to help, but they need also to develop wisdom in order to deal with each different person's situation. It must have been a week later when I received a card from this couple thanking me and apologizing for the mother's outburst. In my mind there was no need for any apology as I had learned a great lesson – which was to count my blessings that I did not have to carry such pain. Even now, many years on I still send prayers to them and ask that they find peace again.

11

Love Is ...

SINCE I am so frequently asked it, let me return to the question of whether pets go into the Spirit World. Yes, yes, yes, and they frequently come through to make their presence felt.

At the end of his life our beloved Charlie developed leukaemia and I had to have him put to sleep. At the vet's I took him through all his life and the vet was laughing as I said, 'Do you remember this, Charlie?' and, 'Do you remember that?' Then, when I'd reached a point where I knew he was happy, I told the vet, 'Do it now.' She couldn't understand why I had chosen that particular moment. It was because I wanted his last memories of life on this earth to be happy ones.

Now, I recently went back to Scotland to pack up some stuff when we were selling the house. Suddenly I had a vision of Charlie running up to the window and then I could feel him rubbing against my legs like he always used to. I gathered up all his pictures, put them in the car and told him, 'Right, you're not staying up here, you're coming to London with me.' And I know he will come through to me again and again and he is always happy. Incidentally, I didn't need to collect those items for Charlie's benefit – that was for me. As I have already endeavoured to explain, the Spirit does not need material things. All I was doing was collecting objects which would act like keys to unlock my mind from time to time, so that I could play back living memories of my old friend.

We have an animals' service at the church in Notting Hill every summer and all the money that gets raised goes to Care for the Wild and other animal charities. One woman even brought a python. The funny thing is, no pets ever behave badly during that service. It never ceases to amaze me how much love we have for our animals while people can be so destructive to each other.

I have written a lot on earlier pages about love: from the love that those who are grieving feel they have lost, to the love that sometimes leaves us on this side, such as when Kate and I went our separate ways. It all begs the question, 'What is love?'

I see love as chemistry between two beings. At first it's an all-consuming passion when you at your best meet someone else at their best, the good feelings in you blending with the good feelings in them. If we are realistic we accept that that state of euphoria cannot last for ever before it starts to change – or perhaps 'diminish' might be a more appropriate word. Then, whatever you try to do about it, the bits of you you never wanted the other person to see – perhaps anger and neurosis figure in there somewhere – start to emerge. And that's when 'love' is tested. Can you both get over the differences that ensue? Is your friendship deep enough to survive this change in the relationship? Remember, love is not a constant in this physical world; it's something that flows through us if and when we are ready to accept it.

Why do I divert from the theme of this book to say that? Because most of the time it is love – often unrequited – that draws people to those they have lost. When people die, love is almost always the unfinished business they leave behind. I am thinking especially of a woman who questioned me from the audience at the Royal Concert Hall in Glasgow last April. She was clearly happy when I gave her messages from her mother, whose death seemed to have locked her in a time warp. But she sobbed her heart out as she asked her final question: 'Does she still love me?' 'Yes,' her mother replied, 'absolutely.' No unfinished business there then. My heart was in my mouth as I passed that on. What a wonderful thing it is to be able to do something like that.

*****

THROUGHOUT this book I have tried to relay how I see my role in life as helping those who grieve. So many of us waste huge chunks of our lives by allowing ourselves to be consumed by grief when someone close to us passes over. That is hard to get through to a mother who has lost, say, a teenage son, because it is natural, totally natural, for her to wonder what he would have looked like in middle age, whether he would have become a father and what his children would have looked like.

But there comes a point when that's *all* she will think, and she regards it as her destiny so to do. No-one comes into this world to spend the latter half of their life grieving: that woman was more than just a mother to her son, she is also, or has been, a daughter herself, a wife, a member of a community – other roles that she needs to rediscover, and she can only do that by realising that her son wants that for her. People don't die to hurt us – we hurt because they die.

That's why I think that funerals are important for the *living*. They're the letting-go occasion. I am asked to conduct a lot of funerals these days and I consider it an honour. It's a very important day in the lives of those who are left behind and they are the ones who need help on that day. I do what I can to make them realize that by choosing hymns or songs that the one who has passed over enjoyed, they are already demonstrating faith that the Spirit is there with them, there to enjoy his or her favourite tunes and memories. The Spirit is still very much alive. The ceremony is not for the benefit of the deceased; what is being buried or cremated is just dead flesh. Nevertheless, make it a good funeral because it's a tribute that *you* will never forget, I tell them. Be a part of the event but see it as a sending-off and give them good thoughts to go with them, not sad ones.

Sylvia Browne tells a story about her father's passing and how she was virtually blackmailed by the funeral parlour into buying an expensive coffin. In a moment of weakness, perhaps, she said, 'Okay, I loved my father so I'll buy him the best,' and at that point the undertaker said, 'Well, we also have that one lead-lined which means it will never let in water.' And, drawing a line, Sylvia said, 'Would that be in case he drowns? Screw you, I'll take the first one!'

People think that by spending a lot of money and making regular visits to the burial site they are doing something good, whereas what they are really doing is creating a shrine that causes them to be attached to the dead instead of letting go of them. They become attached to a big monument or a hole in the ground just so they can go there and cry, and that's not healthy either for them or for the Spirit of the one who has passed over. Of course it's appropriate to cry when you suffer such a loss, but it's also part of your human nature to survive. There's not a God who says, 'Stand there and cry, you are being a good widow crying for five years, whereas that woman over there is less good because she got over her loss in a year. You are better than her because you cried more.' That's silly. It's self-abuse, self-torture.

Albert Best donated his body to medical science and two years later the hospital wanted to know what we wanted done with the bits they hadn't used. Some people were demanding we hold a service but I said, 'Don't be stupid, it's just remains, get it cremated. That was just a body that Albert used until he didn't need it any more, so just press a button and let the real Albert get on with his life in the Spirit world.'

We did have a brief service of committal at the crematorium, which was hilarious. The man who ran the place (his motto was 'You kill 'em and we'll grill 'em') was in a terrible hurry and when we told him we wanted to sing the hymn *Amazing Grace*, he said, 'I'm very short of time – can you just do half? Do the Amazing and leave out the Grace.' We were in hysterics and, knowing Albert, I'm sure he would have been too.

I tell people at funerals I conduct that the best way to remember someone is to talk through and enjoy really happy memories of them. Happy living memories are the best tribute you can pay to someone who has passed over, not going back time and time again to sob over a piece of ground beneath which their discarded mortal remains are buried – and that applies to pets too, by the way.

As I have written, when my beloved Uncle Michael died I sat and recreated as much of his life in my mind as I could in a short time and sent him those memories, and then I got on with my life – that's what he would have wanted and that's what he got.

I have told both my sons that when I pass into the next world they should not get hung up on this death thing, it would be such an insult to me and the memory of my life. 'Don't do that,' I have said to Paul and Steven. 'It's insulting to who I am and what I have tried to do. Think of all the funny things and laugh. Laugh and be sure I will be there laughing with you. If you were to sit there crying – sinking into the depression that grief turns into – then it would make it so difficult for me to pick you up, and I've got a big journey to make.'

To live every day as if it might be your last is to know freedom from the fear of death. I knew of one old chap – he was 86 – who had cancer but wanted to go to Africa, and someone said to him, 'That's very risky, you might die there,' and his reply was, 'Well, at least I will have *been* there.'

*****

IMAGINE this if you will: a woman (and this happened in one of the American cities I was visiting) went out on a necessary shopping trip leaving her husband lying desperately ill in his bed. He had cancer and was in dreadful pain. When she returned to the house, he had passed. One year to the day following his death she came to a public meeting I was addressing and her husband came through with a message for her. It was full of joy and gratitude. He was fine, he no longer suffered and he was so pleased with the way things had happened. Then he said something puzzling: 'Never tell our daughters our secret.'

I saw the lady afterwards in the tearoom of the hall the meeting had taken place in and she engaged me in conversation. I said there was one other thing that had come up in the message that I had not relayed: he was showing me a box, a box of tablets, and saying she was not to feel bad.

Can you guess the rest? The woman told me that before she had set out on her shopping trip, he had pleaded with her to leave his tablets by the bed. Too weak even to unfasten the top he had asked her to do that too. 'I obliged, Gordon, even though his intention was clear. I loved him so much I couldn't bear for his suffering to go on.'

He had taken the tablets, all of them, but no-one ever knew whether they had brought about his death or whether his time had come anyway. And who was I to judge? Here had been a man who was desperately ill and a wife tormented by his agony. He had come back to give her a very clear message: 'You took away my pain and now I'm well and happy. Never have any thought of guilt again.'

The woman was delighted with his message and went away happy for the first time in a year. As a medium my job is just to pass the message, not to consider the rights and wrongs.

*****

NOT everyone on this side wants to have contact with someone from the Other Side. I was quite taken aback by an old woman who swore (and this was in church) when her husband came through. It was a Sunday evening and everyone seemed very touched when I brought first her father and then her mother through. They gave her plenty of evidence and some very loving sentiments. 'Oh lovely,' she cooed. 'Yes, that's my mum all right.' Then I told her I sensed a man who was reluctant to give his name. Her face hardened. I said, 'He seems almost reluctant, shy even, to come through. Now he's telling me his name is Peter and I sense that he's trying to say sorry.'

The whole congregation looked stunned when she said in a very loud voice, 'Well, you can tell him to get [expletive deleted] back to wherever he's been hiding. That bastard gave me the hardest life any woman could have. He was mean, he was nasty and the day he died I thought I was rid of him and he's got no business coming back. Tell him to [expletive deleted]!'

A moment's silence followed and then the entire congregation burst out laughing. I said, 'Okay, he's got the message. Now let me try and get your mother and father back again if I can.' I succeeded but then Peter came back in again. 'You've got a dog,' I said to the woman, 'a very sick dog.' She agreed and then I continued: 'Peter says it was his dog and he wants you to know he's trying to help where the dog's health is concerned.'

After the service she approached me and said, 'Well, he did love that dog, but he was a bastard to me and I'm not ready to talk to him. I thought when he died he was gone forever and I'd hate to think that when I die I might have to meet him again.'

There was a similar situation when I gave a woman in America a message from her father. 'He wants to apologize to you,' I said. But the woman froze and however much I implored her to respond – 'Please talk to me; he says his name is John, does this make sense to you?' – she would not. 'Oh well,' I said. 'I can't communicate for you if you don't want to receive the message.' I sensed there was much she had to say but did not wish to do so in public and it's not a medium's job to get anyone to do that.

Later I saw her privately and she told me that her father had abused her as a child and she too felt a release when he died and she didn't want to go over the past because it just produced painful memories. But once again I say that very often that's wrong. If something is not cleared up at the time we do have to go back into the past and deal with things, usually with another person, in order to let go of them. If you can seriously walk away from bad memories, then that's fine; but if you harbour anger within you, that can be so destructive, not only to you but also to those around you.

I understood why this lady did not want to deal with this in public but I strongly recommended that she found someone else – another medium, a priest or a professional counsellor – to share her awful memory with. Maybe one day she will be ready to take an apology from her father on the Other Side, but in the meantime she needed to be rid of the hate she carried in her heart.

*****

SO how can we best show love? I don't mean the passionate sort between life partners, but love for our fellow beings while they are still in this world. By giving them time, that's how. In times when we may be grumbling about our lot in life it shows us how much we've got and how little some others have. I used to cut hair for the down-and-outs at a place called the Legion of Mary. They were mainly alcoholics and every time I put a glass of my favourite whisky to my lips I think about those poor people and say, 'There but for the Grace of God …'

They were men and women who had just resigned themselves to a life on the streets. It is amazing to see how the human spirit can be broken, disconnected at some point, never to be repaired. In many cases it is as futile as an amputee hoping to grow a new leg. All those of us who worked there could do was to throw them a scrap of dignity by cleaning them up. They were actually just waiting for death, and when they reach that stage they are totally passive.

I learned a lot from these people. Because I was just a barber cutting hair and not an authority figure, they opened up and talked about their lives. One particular evening I was thinking, *Oh God, I need to get my house sorted*, when this old boy came up to me. When he saw I was packing up he said, 'Oh, I'm really sorry,' and started to move away. I said, 'Come here and let me cut your hair.' Though he didn't know it he was ridding me of the high-class problem about my house. 'No, no, son,' he said. 'It's okay.' I actually had to coax him into the chair.

His name was John and his story was typical. After his children had left home, his wife died and he was left with no purpose in life and no-one to help him through the grief because he didn't want to be 'a burden' to his children. Paralysed by that grief, he could not find the means to pay his rent and got put into a shelter. He didn't get on with the people there and ended up wandering the streets spending every penny he had on booze to sedate himself.

How differently things might have turned out for John had he been able to connect with his wife in the Spirit world and receive her encouraging words to get on with his life. How often I find myself having to deliver that message. How many Johns there might have been.

When I asked him what he wished for, it was a simple request: 'I just hope that I can die in a bed and not on the street.' When a man's sole desires come down to that, it puts everything into perspective.

John blames no-one for his condition, but that is often not the case with alcoholics I come across. In trouble for something they've done they say, 'I would never have done that unless I was drunk or high.' Now that's rubbish because it's saying, 'I could never get angry if I didn't drink.' We can all get fraught with or without drink and sometimes the cold anger of sobriety is worse.

When I am carrying a message from the Spirit world to someone who has a drink problem – perhaps a woman who has passed telling her husband that he is imbibing too much – I never get a denial from the recipient. A psychoplogist who wanted to see what I did asked if he could accompany me on one occasion. Afterwards he said: 'My God, it sometimes takes those in my profession months to get people to admit that they are drinking alcoholically or taking so-called social drugs, but you get there in a matter of minutes. It can also take forever to get someone to admit that they are angry, but not in your case.'

I pointed out the difference: 'In your job you can't tell them they are angry, you have to wait for them, to tell you. In mine the Spirits cut to the chase and tell them, and few deny the Spirits the truth. There would be no point to that.'

The analyst doesn't know where the anger or depression started and it can take many, many sessions of therapy to draw it out, but the Spirit knows and can pinpoint it in a matter of moments. It saves a lot of time and it's cheaper than the Priory!

*****

I FIND myself constantly reviewing my own life. After all, how can I help others if my own house is not in order? And I am aware that the greatest pain I have ever suffered came about as a result of my reluctance to admit the truth at the time of my unnecessarily prolonged marriage break-up. It caused Kate, Paul and Steven to suffer too. Whenever I went back to the house to see the boys – and it was practically every evening – when it was time to go, Steven would say, 'Dad, why don't you just stay tonight? Why are you going away again?' And both boys would just stand and look at me – wondering where I was going.

Even though I was coming back the next day, the pain of it was deep because it felt like a betrayal of my children even though I had not left Kate for anyone else. I had to work on that. Was my life going to be this emotional thing with strings from me to Kate, to Paul and to Steven? Should we all just sit together, laugh in our good moods and cry in bad? Or is there another purpose to it? Another purpose to feeling things, hurting? No pain, no gain indeed.

One of the greatest purposes to life is to feel feelings. That's what brings about change and if nothing changes, nothing changes. I had to go through those experiences; we all have to do that if we are to grow.

For me the message was, 'If you shut that door and live a lie for the rest of your life you will be miserable and you will inflict ongoing misery on others. When you have to let go of something or someone, just let go. The landing will be softer than you think.'

*****

HATRED is such a destructive emotion, but thankfully the Spirits can turn that around for us. I have written before of the American lawyer, Richard, whose daughter committed suicide after her fiancé was murdered. The family was badly damaged, and his son changed from a beautiful, peaceable young man into an angry one.

When Richard came to me I was able to put him in touch with his daughter, and her message to him was, 'This can all be reconnected, there is a way of putting it all back together again. Don't let hate blacken your heart.'

Now since then Richard has been back to see me and although I don't often see people more than once, since he had travelled all the way from America I felt obliged to do what I could. This time the message seemed to have no great bearing on his suffering: he would be in Virginia talking about crime. 'Gordon,' he said with his lawyer's hat on, 'I have no business to conduct in Virginia and I am not a criminal lawyer.'

I didn't hear from him again until he phoned me some time later – from Virginia. He had been summoned to Washington from an overseas holiday. Now, he was frequently in Washington on business but it was always an internal flight which lands within the city boundaries.

The international airport, however, is outside the city – in the state of Virginia.

'I can't believe this,' he said, 'though I should do because you told me it was going to happen. And on my arrival I was asked to give a talk on the victims of crime on which, of course, I have become something of an expert from personal experience.'

He delivered the speech and started to visit prisons where he would ask the inmates, 'How do you feel about what you've done?' One day during the course of this he found himself confronted by the killers of the brilliant young man with whom his daughter had been so much in love she could not face life on earth without him; and as a result of her suicide his son had been emotionally ruined and his emotional life torn apart.

'But do you know what, Gordon?' he said. 'I found I didn't hate them. I did hate them once, I swore I would kill them if ever I got the chance. But today I just saw them as teenage boys who'd got into trouble. What brought about this change?'

I knew exactly what had done that: his daughter's 'Don't let hate blacken your heart' message from the Spirit world. The Higher Power who supervises all this stuff is not a punishing God but one who tells us, in one way or another, 'You have to take this on board, otherwise you're never going to move up that Bell Jar, you're going to be stuck in the mud at the bottom of the pond.' He would have sent the same message to those guys who killed Richard's son-in-law-to-be, saying 'Look at what you've done, you've not just killed this person for a pair of trainers, but you've destroyed two whole families, and here is this man whose heart you would expect to be full of hate, talking to you and showing you that he doesn't hate you.'

Everyone, no matter what he or she does in their life, has the chance to rise to the top of that pond and blossom above it instead of being stuck under the mud and filth. Nobody stops you but you. Some people, however intelligent, are terribly ignorant on matters like this. Not because they want to be but because they are. I urge anyone who gets a message from the Spirit world to examine it closely and look for layers beneath it. It may help you on some occasion in the future, just like it did Richard Rosen.

*****

QUITE recently I was asked if I have ever received a message from the late and (as I've endeavoured to point out) much-loved Albert Best. It reminded me that indeed I had and, as you might expect, the circumstances were most extraordinary.

The last time I was to see Albert fully conscious, prior to seeing him on his deathbed and hearing his last words, Jim and I paid him a visit to take him something we had bought him. It was a wet afternoon and we were both wearing raincoats, so I suppose we looked the parts we were about to play. When we arrived there was a strange woman with him in his sitting room. That in itself was not unusual because Albert often had people call on him for impromptu sittings and half the time he had never set eyes on that person before. But there was something different about this one.

Albert introduced Jim and me to the woman as Detective Inspector McManus and Detective Sergeant Coltrane. We had no idea what this was all about but when Albert winked at me I thought, *Okay, this woman is trying to con him and he wants her to believe that we are policemen.* She immediately started to pack up a pile of jewellery – clearly of the costume type – she had spread out on the table and said she would be on her way. I said to Albert that we had to leave too and we would see the lady out.

On the way she asked us a series of questions like how long we'd been on the force. We both felt stupid but made up answers that seemed to satisfy her inquisitiveness.

Soon afterwards Albert suffered a stroke and I never did get the opportunity to ask him what all that was about and we never did see his 'visitor' again. Some two months after he died, I received a social visit at the Spiritualist church in Notting Hill from an American medium, Larry Taylor, who lived opposite the church. Although there was no particular reason for his visit, during the course of it he remembered something he thought I should hear: 'I've got a message for you,' he said. 'I was meditating the other day when the Spirit of Albert Best came through. He was pointing in a certain direction and when I opened my eyes I saw it was the writing bureau he was indicating. He wanted me to write something down. I got a sheet of paper and wrote what he said – it means nothing to me but perhaps it does to you.'

And with that he produced a crumpled envelope from his pocket and handed it to me.

I opened it and read in amazement what my American friend had written down. It said, 'My best wishes to the two detectives.'

Nobody but Jim or I could have known about the incident that inspired that message. It's things like that which help sustain my faith.

12

Where Do We Go From Here?

RARELY has a Spirit come back through me more than once, but one young man paid four visits – three of them within 24 hours. I was giving a demonstration at the Spiritualist church in Notting Hill on a Saturday night in October 2005 when I received a message for a couple sat at the back of the church. I had never seen them before but it was obvious that they were in great pain. I told them, 'You've lost a son and he's coming through to give me all kinds of information. He says he died in a van, a white van, and it was very recent,' and the man agreed – their son had been killed in a road accident just four weeks earlier.

'He's telling me he lived in Shepherd's Bush but he died on a motorway. [Again affirmative nods.] He says he's sorry that you are grieving so much but he is fine.'

He was so buoyant, so full of energy, this boy, and he gave them this amazing message, the crux of which was that they should stop crying over him and see him as being alive. He told them of things he had done around the house to try and make them aware of his presence – like making the radio come on to what had been his favourite station with a piece of the black music he had grown so fond of.

His mother and father – Joanne and Wayne Burford are their names – said they had thought it was him but until that moment they could never be sure. It was one of those really happy and joyous messages.

The following morning I was taking the Sunday service and in the front row there was a group of women, and I started to give them a message. I said, 'There's a young man here ... wait a moment, this sounds familiar. Do you have family who were here last night because this sounds to me like the same guy who came through last night? He's saying he died last month, on September 8, and that his name is George.'

They did indeed have family who were there the previous night. This was George's sister Michelle and sister-in-law. He gave me all kinds of information, various names and dates and then he said, 'Something of mine is going to be returned to you,' and they looked at me like I was crazy. He also mentioned somebody having had a tattoo done. Well, Dan, one of his brothers, had apparently had a likeness of George tattooed over his heart.

That night I was back in church for the evening service and there was a group of young men there I hadn't seen before. They seemed to stand out, even though the church was packed. They turned out to be George's brother Dan and some friends. I learned later that Dan had done everything possible to avoid going to the church because he was an out-and-out non-believer in Spiritualism; but I understand he changed like Saul on the road to Damascus when I told him that George was taking off something from around his neck and giving it back to him. It wasn't until afterwards I was told that George had always worn a gold chain belonging to Dan.

So he came back three times on two successive days and if that wasn't enough he came through yet again two months later to deliver a message via me to a woman at the SAGB. Because I was so familiar with him by now, I asked her if she was a relative of George Burford's. Not a relative, she said, but one of his neighbours and a close friend of the family. On that occasion he mentioned the name Buster as evidence for her. I thought it might be a dog but she told me it was actually the name of another of George's brothers – yet another thing I could not possibly have known, of course.

George was a brilliant communicator. I saw his mother again recently and she said, 'You've no idea how much that helped me. The night I came back from the church I got my first night's sleep since George died.' That was nice because I don't often get feedback. It made it all seem worthwhile,

And as for the thing of his he had promised his mother and father would be returned to them? Joanne let me know later that the following January, one of his friends turned up at their house saying, 'I've come to bring back George's Gucci shoes, he left them at my place.'

*****

EARLIER this year (2006) I gave up my hairdressing business to devote myself full-time to my work as a medium. It simply got harder and harder to juggle both things. People would slip into the salon and, edging closer and closer to me while I was cutting somebody's hair, would eventually say something like, 'Do you feel it?' and, perhaps a little irritably on occasions, I would say, 'Feel what?' They would perhaps tell me that they had just lost their father and I would say, 'No, I'm sorry, I don't sense him. I'm cutting hair.' Some would persist: 'Yes, I know what you're doing but you must sense him.' And that's when it began to get unbearable – especially when it was a woman who had brought her husband in and, seeing he hadn't got the guts to say what he had been instructed to, would come and stand behind me and say, 'You're that psychic guy, aren't you? My husband's mother died last week; can you put him in touch with her?'

Others would wait until we were closing the shop and they'd duck in, saying, 'I waited until you closed; I hope you don't mind this intrusion but I need to see you,' and I'd have to explain that I had a normal life to lead and had plans of my own for the evening. 'But shall we just wait then?' they would say, seemingly oblivious to the answer I had already given. 'Come and speak to me at the Spiritualist church,' I would say, but many of them wouldn't dream of setting foot in a place that wasn't of their religion.

Even that didn't stop some. Some – and I accept that these were desperate people – tried emotional blackmail. One of our girl hairdressers phoned me in tears one day saying that a man was at the door threatening to kill himself unless I promised that very night to go and see his wife who was crippled with grief over the loss of their son. I was in London at the time but the man was having none of it: 'Well, if you don't reach him and get him to my wife without delay then you will be responsible for her death,' he concluded.

It's just bad behaviour to put that on a shop assistant. People say to me, 'And how do you know how you would behave if you were in that man's position?' I only hope that I would conduct myself in such a way that I would not throw emotional punishment for my dilemma on a poor girl. When we are hurting it's important that we check our behaviour and don't lash out at others. A few grieving people do take that stance: 'I want answers and if I don't get them, you're going to hurt too.' And that's why the grievers often get ignored by others. You don't know what to say for the best; we don't like it when we are faced with something we can't do anything about. On many occasions I have encountered parents who have lost a child pushing the guilt on to a surviving child. It's the old 'Now look what you made me do' we got from our mothers when they broke something. The complications that families have through guilt are horrendous and that's why we need to learn how to deal with it. That's what I try and teach.

But I was determined to follow Albert Best's advice and not go down the same path as he had trodden. Albert never knew how what he did worked. I thought that he would have great answers to all the questions that were whirring round in my head, but he didn't. Now I look back I think that was not a sad thing but a great thing, because even this great medium had no idea what it was all about. And he never really wanted to know.

Losing his family in the way that he did propelled Albert into a life of total self-sacrifice. He was amazing at helping people, especially those who had lost kids. It was really exciting to know him. He was something else, a very grounded man. I remember him telling me, 'Gordon, please don't be like me, I don't want you to do all the things I've done. I know you have something you can give to people, but don't let people take you with it because that's what I've done all my life. And as for the so-called important ones, they wouldn't let you in the back door if you didn't have the Gift.'

Alas, Albert was never able to act on his own advice. People, strangers even, would turn up on his doorstep at midnight and he would see them. It was almost like a penance, like he was duty-bound to help people, yet he constantly said to me, 'Have a life as well, don't just be a medium.' That was one of the most important messages I ever got from him, to be myself and stop trying to heal the world.

'Just help who you can,' he said, 'and don't go over the top.' He himself never knew when to say no and he never stopped, and it was not because he didn't want to. He couldn't say no to them because he thought if he did he was letting them down. I have learned to say no.

*****

THERE are odd occasions when I am unable to resist a heart-felt plea for a sitting but, as I have said before, money is never an issue. I never ever accept a penny for being able to use my Gift to help some grief-stricken person in a sitting. When I was working in South Africa my son Paul came to me and said a woman and her son were prepared to pay thousands of dollars to sit down privately with me. Paul knew perfectly well I wouldn't accept the money but he said, 'Dad, they must be terribly sad to go to these lengths,' so I agreed somehow to try and fit a sitting into the schedule.

The only problem was that this was in Johannesburg and I was about to leave for Cape Town. They said, 'No problem, we'll fly anywhere.'

The following day they turned up at my hotel room in Cape Town and during the hour-long sitting they got a most comforting message from the woman's son (the boy's brother, of course) who had been killed in an accident. He gave lots of positive evidence that it was indeed him but the bulk of it was about the surviving brother's recent wedding. The Spirit said he'd been there, he'd laughed at some of the speeches and greatly enjoyed the fact that they had drunk a toast to him.

They were so grateful at the end that again they tried to insist on recompensing me. I told them the happy smiles on their faces more than sufficed. Some months later I was driving up to my home when I noticed a strange car on the driveway. On the doorstep were two friends of the people I had seen. They were on holiday in the UK and had driven hundreds of miles out of their way to deliver some South African wine from the pair I had seen in Cape Town.

How could I refuse?

*****

GRIEVING is very much learning to deal with change. Until we understand and develop a sense of spiritual faith, the loss of a loved one will always seem like the biggest change of all. But a lot of people suffer unnecessarily in this life because they cannot, will not, allow themselves to cope with change, and I think it is very important from a healing point of view to look at this.

The natural reaction to change is to resist it, to be fearful of it (there's that word again!). That applies from the small changes – when we are kids and have to change schools, for example – right up until we have to change jobs or lose somebody. Those who adjust are the people who have little or no fear in their lives: they can accept moving on.

Unlike plants, we are not rooted in this earth, we are the moving vehicle and when we have to, we move with events.

Some years ago I was cutting a boy's hair and his mother was complaining that she had to put their house on the market that day, and she dreaded the prospect of hordes of people traipsing through it as a result. I asked her where it was and it was quite a nice area, so I said to Jim, 'Do you fancy us buying a house?' The woman stared at me in disbelief and said, 'You are joking, aren't you?' I assured her I was not; we took a look at it that night and bought it there and then.

Eighteen months later Jim asked me to take some videos back to the shop. As I was passing a house on the way, a man was putting a For Sale sign up in the garden of his beautiful bungalow. I stopped his car and asked, 'How much do you want for your house, mate?' Now it was more than we could afford but I believe that change is also about taking some chances in life. We bought it and I was sitting there one day thinking, *Have we over-extended ourselves? No, I know I've done the right thing; something will come along, it always does. Something's going to happen that will change my life*. Anyway, I took Charlie out for his walk and sent a thought out to the universe: *I know something's about to change, can you please hurry up with it?* and when I got back there was a message from Michelle Pilley saying that the American publishers Hay House were setting up in Britain and would I like to write a book for them? (This is now the fourth, by the way.) Now the most bizarre element of this story is that the night before Michelle's call I dreamed I was entering a house made with bales of straw – a hay house.

*****

MOST people who go to mediums are stuck at a crossroads. And that again is where the Spirits come in, in giving those on this side the go-ahead to make the change. I just love to see the look of relief when I pass on a message presenting someone with the opportunity to take the plunge, to make a change. It's permission from the Other Side. People often say that the messages are repetitive but there's a reason for that – their lives are repetitive. People often come to see me because they are stuck, they need a push, and rather than take the responsibility of change they need to be told to do it by someone they respected and trusted. A widow left on her own, for example, might be thinking of moving house but feels she needs her late husband's approval.

The other thing to remember about this is that you have to be confident in life, have trust in your life. Spirits do not experience failure. Confidence is so important and that's very much tied up with trust in the next life. Fear of change is really fear of failure. Trust your inner voice. If it seems right, do it. So many people talk to me about stress and being depressed but most of the time it is simply that they are not prepared to meet change halfway – we all meet changes in our lives every day and if you don't deal with them you are in danger of becoming a stagnant human being.

*****

I REGULARLY look at the fact that I will die (I do this as early in the morning as possible and then I haven't wasted the whole day). Two thoughts on that subject come to mind – if you do smoke and drink, don't worry about it. The worry is more likely to kill you than the alcohol and tobacco. Second, try not to take a heavy overcoat with you – and by that I mean the weight of conscience. Sort things out before you go. If, for instance, you were abusive to people as a result of drinking too much and then found God in your life and thought, 'Oh, God has saved me,' that's not enough. You need to have done something to correct your karma, your actions. No 'finding of God' will take away the fact that you committed certain acts that have caused stains on your soul, your conscience. So at some point – whether here or there – you have got to clean it up. I used the phrase 'clear away the wreckage of the past' earlier. That's exactly what you need to do. Make amends where you have caused damage, clean your side of the street no matter what you think anyone has done to you. It will free you of guilt and a life without guilt is a life of freedom.

I can honestly say that I am happy practically every day of my life. I can be ecstatically happy when I meet any member of my family. And when I am working as a medium I get filled up with joy but happiness to me is all about being contented. I'm not looking for highs – they are usually followed by lows. The ultimate thing is to keep balance in your life.

I don't often get sad. I am actually more moved by somebody's bravery than by somebody dying. Witnessing someone overcoming some huge hurdle in their life is for me a far more emotional experience than watching somebody die, because death is a natural thing: it calls for no great act of courage.

And when it comes to stress, people say, for example, that moving house is enormously stressful. What's stressful about it? It's only stressful if you make it so, if you challenge it.

As I have already stated – go with the flow or life will be so much more difficult. And try not to take on other people's pain. That's like saying, 'Where's my cross?' You simply cannot help others out of the mud if you're down there in it with them.

When you are doing anything of a Spiritual nature you have a chance to develop two things – one is wisdom, the other is compassion, and one is no good without the other. If you are kind but unwise, foolishly kind, you will give just for the sake of giving. You try and please everybody but you have no boundaries to protect yourself. Foolish and kind people say things like 'I've been a giver all my life and nobody ever gave back to me.' That is kindness or compassion without wisdom.

A person with wisdom but no compassion, on the other hand, is somebody who is selfishly intellectual, who refuses to share that wisdom. To do things in order to be seen doing them is all about ego. That's being wise and not compassionate.

To do something for the right reasons – balancing compassion and wisdom – is all about positive action. That's all very Tibetan of course and although I have not studied Buddhism, I seem to understand its philosophy instinctively. I have been fortunate enough to meet lamas who will not be seen in public and they have sent me things, which have been very helpful in my own pursuit of all things Spiritual.

*****

IT is often hard to know why we make the choices we do that can lead us into terrible situations. Frances, a cousin of mine, was killed because she made what might be considered a wrong choice. But was it?

Frances had been at her sister's house and the two of them had a tiff, so Frances walked out. The two of them did a lot of the same things and they had identical raincoats, and when Frances left the house in a huff she took her sister's by mistake. She realized this but didn't want to go back to her sister's house, so she called her brother who would have driven her home – but she couldn't get through to him. Instead she called a taxi. When she got to the house she realized that the keys were in her raincoat at her sister's. She had two choices – to go to her brother's and stay the night or to go back to her sister's, get the correct raincoat with the keys in the pocket and sleep in her own bed. She chose the latter. At that point a private car came along that she thought was a taxi. She got into it and was murdered.

Frances has come back to me several times. She told me – via a medium who happened to be visiting the church one night – that I would find out more about what happened to her from police reports that were coming to me. I thought, *That's rubbish – how would I ever get a confidential police report on Frances Barker's death?* But she was not wrong. Unbeknownst to me, John, my boss at a city barber's, used to write for the magazine *True Detective*. I happened to be telling him one night about Frances's death and he said, 'Wait a minute, I think I've got the police report on that murder case ...' – they let him see confidential reports and photographs of the corpses for his writing – and he went home and found it. The family weren't told the gruesome details. But here they were in the report Frances had told me I would see. It also contained information about a gold compact that the killer had given to his daughter saying he had bought it from

Woolworth's. I knew that that was a reference to just such an item which Frances's brother had given her.

*****

I BELIEVE that Frances chose the route that led to her brutal death. Why, you may ask, would anyone want to take on such pain? To do it from a human point of view makes no sense, but I look at it from a Spiritual viewpoint. Now, this some people will find hard to understand, but I accept the teaching that we choose our path in this life before we enter it. I believe therefore that my cousin will have put herself up there for what happened, as indeed her killer would have done.

The thinking goes like this: you come onto this earth to burn up karma and you do that through suffering and other emotional life experiences. To rise higher in the Bell Jar or the pond, you need to do that. Karma is just action, so burning up karma is burning up your actions. So instead of a life of grace and serenity you choose a life in which you will have many emotional experiences, go through a horrendous marriage or suffer brutality because you cannot get those things in the Spirit world.

Here on earth we find it hard to come to terms with physical failures, physical and mental disabilities and tragedies such as murder. They make us exclaim, 'Oh, my God, how awful is that. Why me? I haven't done anything to deserve that.' It's like my cousin's mother saying, 'But I haven't done anything wrong to deserve my daughter being killed,' and she'd be quite right to say that; but at some point in her Spirit life she would have decided that she needed to take on such pain – and the same goes for those around her, including Frances. People live defining moments in this life and I believe we set them up for ourselves before we come here. That's why we have free will when you join another time line. Say, for example, that there are three ways to get to London from any given point and on the route that you choose various things happen to you along the way. Two other people who chose the other routes reach the same destination but when they get there they describe different happenings. You say, 'I was going to go that way, I wanted to go that way which would have given me the experiences you had.' But remember you *chose* the route you took and that, I believe, is the same with our lives and our life experiences.

So we need to remember that we made our life choices from a Spiritual point of view.

As a human being who is experiencing suffering you might well say, 'Why would I choose that? I would never have chosen that.' Yes, you did, you chose it because you wanted to burn off karma in order to feel enlightened.

Sometimes we reach junctions of time lines in which we get glimpses of our future. This happened to the prophets, of course, at times in their lives. They were men specially gifted with this ability. This often results in self-fulfilling prophecies – things happen because we have seen they are likely to in those glimpses of the future. We have been steered in their direction. But beware of self-*destroying* prophecies: *Will my son get home safely from the disco tonight; I feel someone's going to hurt him.* That's not a glimpse of the future, that's paranoia and it will harm you, not your son. In the same way you can hold yourself back from enjoying the day if you think, *If I get too happy I will have to pay for it and all this will be taken away from me.* Don't be afraid to savour your happiness.

*****

I RECEIVE a great deal of learning from the Spirit world – not necessarily individual Spirits but from the force that is all around them, and indeed us, if we only heed it. Before I left my Scottish home for London recently, I had an amazing experience during a walk with my dog in the hills by my home on the shore near Loch Lomond. It was a windy day and I had sat down for a few moments beside a waterfall. I could feel the grass moving and the sound of the trickling waterfall was far, far louder than I had ever heard it. It was a feeling of being in touch with nature, and with it came what I can only describe as an experience of great clarity, of reassurance, of everything in my world being okay.

The message I was getting was, 'You are fine and you are where you are meant to be. The chaos you think surrounds you is about to be replaced by a feeling of utter calm.'

At that moment I realized that we are very powerful. The problem is that we are often too scared to explore the realms that have been opened up to us. How insignificant we can become in this world if we fail to see the potential we have as Spirit beings. We become dependent on another person, a house, a car, a job or a drink and we overlook the religion of our own self, which allows us to become part of this life force, this God force, and that is infinitely more valuable.

I have been brought to understand that God is actually the life we live, the electricity which fuels *everything*.

What does 'made in the image of God' mean? It has nothing to do with being a person, there is no old man up there in the sky who resembles us, it's to do with being part of life or light. To use our lives in the best possible way and to be as natural as everything else in this world – like that waterfall. Go with the flow. Go against it and it will probably kill you, not because it wants to, but it is in its nature to carry you with it and not to allow you to resist it.

Often we become stuck when we ourselves are in the mid-stream of life but frightened to let it carry us safely along. So we stay there, disconnected and isolated. That's when people become human and less Spiritual, so dense, solid and fearful. Then, when we go with the flow of life, we become joyous and in harmony with nature. That's the moment people are inclined to say, 'I'm in love.'

It's important to recognize that another person cannot give you love, only to inspire the love that is in you. People who complain they have never been in love have not learned to love themselves. How can anyone else love you if you do not love who and what you are? Don't blame life for lack of love; blame yourself for not allowing love to rise in you. Love is there all the time if you go to it, just like the mountains and waterfalls are always there.

Each and every one of us is given a key to open the door to a full and happy life – all we have to do is place it in the lock and turn it, but we are often afraid to do so. There is nothing that big, nothing that bad that can't be dealt with if we are prepared to go with the flow. The message I get time and time again to pass on from the Spirits is if you love someone in this life – your children, say – then don't let fear hold that back by telling yourself something awful is going to happen to them. Meet life head on and go wherever it takes you.

We cannot stand alone as islands in the stream and say, 'I can't deal with that, I can't move on.' As I described earlier, people who fear close down and become human, and when we're human is when we're at our worst. It's when we act badly, sacrificing our emotional intelligence. Human emotions are just surface emotions. We need to go deeper and find the Spirit within. It will change your entire life. Sure, we are meant to shape ourselves and that can involve pain.

Sitting by that waterfall that windy day I realized that the pains of life are the pains we must suffer to make ourselves more pure, more clear, more spiritual.

*****

AND where do I go from here? I would like to teach, to develop the philosophy I have learned through my experiences and pass it all on, as I have endeavoured to do on these pages. I am very interested in the works of Carl Jung and Sigmund Freud. Their influence on society has been tremendous. To me it's all about consciousness, about stripping down the mind so it shows the person, not the intellect. Neurosis, for example, is not a part of your spiritual being and it will not travel with your Spiritual being. That stuff belongs in this world.

Although exhilarating, to keep demonstrating my Gift can also be exhausting, and I can see the day coming where it could be self-defeating for me to go on proving it as opposed to telling people what I have learned about life on the Other

Side. I hope I will never stop reuniting the grieving with their loved ones, which is, and always will be, the voluntary part of my work (how could you tell a bereaved mother that her son loves her 'and, by the way, that'll be £50'?). The people I have given messages to have proved to be extraordinarily grateful, but I am grateful too. I have learned from every single experience they have allowed me to share and in one way or another I will always try to be available to those I encounter who are suffering with their grief.

But there is so much more to do and I have been fortunate enough to acquire so much knowledge to pass on. I have been going back into the past with people for most of my life. Looking ahead, making predictions, is often a guess based on my feelings at any given moment, a gut reaction based on whatever sixth sense I have been given. For myself, I rarely look back or forward now. I am most comfortable living in the day, in the moment, and that is a feeling I hope I can leave you with.

About Gordon Smith

Gordon Smith is an astoundingly accurate medium. He is renowned for his ability to give the exact names of people, places and even streets. Gordon travels around the world to appear before audiences, read for celebrities and demonstrate his abilities, but his feet have remained firmly on the ground. Gordon's extraordinary skills have attracted the attention of university scientists researching the paranormal as well as countless journalists and documentary makers.

Gordon Smith's outstanding abilities as a medium, or messenger from the Spirit world, have brought comfort and healing to thousands of people worldwide.

Find Out More
If you're interested in finding out more about Gordon – his books, his life and his personal appearances – visit his official website: **www.psychicbarber.com**.

Sign up online for his newsletter and you'll be the first to be informed about new dates added to his schedule. You'll also receive free downloads and lots more!

'amazing' Time Out

'What I have is a gift, a gift that must not be abused for self-gain, but must be given freely to those whose need is greatest and who will benefit most from it.' Gordon Smith

You could be one of a lucky few to win a one-to-reading with Gordon Smith. If you are interested in entering this competition, log on to Gordon's official website to find out more: www.psychicbarber.com.

Other books and products available by Gordon Smith

Spirit Messenger

Read Gordon's first book, *Spirit Messenger*, and find out how he became a medium, what has influenced his spiritual development over the years and what it has been like to work with the scientific world. Full of numerous stories told in Gordon's down-to-earth style, *Spirit Messenger* is the beginning of the journey.

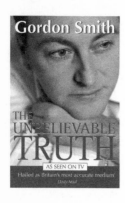

The Unbelievable Truth

In this, Gordon's second book, he answers the questions he is most often asked by the people he meets. Gordon explains how the world of spirit works and how spirits communicate; he covers ghosts, hauntings, out-of-body experiences and much more. Ideal for anyone searching for more information on this huge subject area and a perfect accompaniment to *Through My Eyes* and *Spirit Messenger*.

Through My Eyes

Thousands of people have come to see Gordon seeking
healing. From them he has gained a profound insight into
the true nature of grief and our relationship with the Spirit
world. In this, his third book, you can join Gordon as he
describes the true nature of grief, how it affects us and our
loved ones who have crossed over. An uplifting and
insightful book guaranteed to bring peace of mind to
anyone that has been touched by loss.

Gordon Smith's Introduction to the Spirit World

This is the first CD by Gordon. On CD1 you can hear a live workshop in which Gordon describes his experiences of the Spirit world and his development as a medium. He outlines the ways that the Spirit world make their presence known to their loved ones and explains ways of feeling closer to Spirit. In his matter-of-fact and humorous style Gordon explains some of the mechanics of mediumship and describes how psychics differ from mediums. Listening to this inspirational CD will enable you to gain a closer understanding of the work of a medium and help you to open up a deeper connection to the Spirit world.

CD2 contains three guided meditations:

1. Listening to your inner voice and higher self
2. Connecting to your spirit guides
3. Sending compassion and healing to others

The 5 Keys to Happiness Oracle Cards

This extraordinary deck of oracle cards fuses ancient Tibetan wisdom with contemporary Western psychological insight to give you the keys to achieving a happier and more balanced life. Using the five Tibetan elements of Earth, Water, Fire, Air and Space, this deck will help you understand the elemental forces, of which you and the world around you are composed. Use these 34 cards for daily guidance, individual spreads or for meditation. Also included is a mandala image for guidance in laying out spreads.

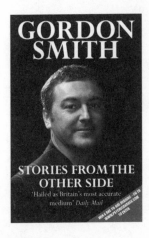

Stories from the Other Side

In his latest and most intimate book Gordon shares his most amazing encounters with the unseen world, as well as revealing much about his own life and his journey to this point. The book includes numerous previously untold stories as you travel with Gordon into churches and theatres around the world, where he connects the bereaved with the Other Side.

Don't forget you can find out more about Gordon Smith, his life, his work and his upcoming personal appearances by visiting his official website: www.psychicbarber.com.

All of the above products are available from all good bookshops or by calling Hay House Publishers on 020 8962 1230.

We hope you enjoyed this Hay House book.
If you would like to receive a free catalogue featuring additional
Hay House books and products, or if you would like information
about the Hay Foundation, please contact:

Hay House UK Ltd
Unit B • 292 Kensal Road • London W10 5BE
Tel: (44) 20 8962 1230; Fax: (44) 20 8962 1239
www.hayhouse.co.uk

****

Published and distributed in the United States of America by:
Hay House, Inc. • P.O. Box 5100 • Carlsbad, CA 92018-5100
Tel: (1) 760 431 7695 or (800) 654 5126; Fax: (1) 760 431 6948 or (800) 650 5115
www.hayhouse.com

****

Published and distributed in Australia by:
Hay House Australia Ltd • 18/36 Ralph St • Alexandria NSW 2015
Tel: (61) 2 9669 4299 • Fax: (61) 2 9669 4144
www.hayhouse.com.au

****

Published and distributed in the Republic of South Africa by:
Hay House SA (Pty) Ltd • PO Box 990 • Witkoppen 2068
Tel/Fax: (27) 11 706 6612 • orders@psdprom.co.za

****

Distributed in Canada by:
Raincoast • 9050 Shaughnessy St • Vancouver, BC V6P 6E5
Tel: (1) 604 323 7100 • Fax: (1) 604 323 2600

****

Sign up via the Hay House UK website to receive the Hay House
online newsletter and stay informed about what's going on with
your favourite authors. You'll receive bimonthly announcements
about discounts and offers, special events, product highlights,
free excerpts, giveaways, and more!

www.hayhouse.co.uk